Life Lessons

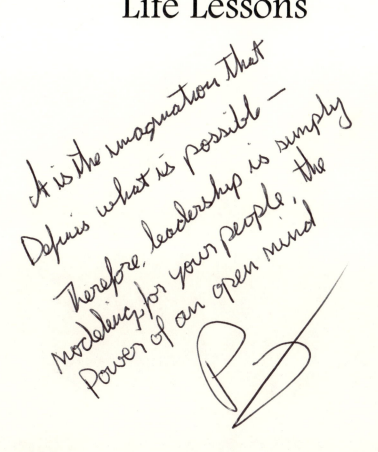

It is the imagination that
Defines what is possible —
Therefore, leadership is simply
modeling for your people, the
Power of an open mind

Life Lessons

*What Experience Teaches Us
About Success*

Perry Pokrandt

Library of Congress Control Number: 2010915554
ISBN: Hardcover   978-1-4535-9962-4
                Softcover   978-1-4535-9961-7
                Ebook   978-1-4535-9963-1

This book was printed in the United States of America.

Foreword and Epilogue by Kristine Pokrandt

To order additional copies of this book, contact:
Xlibris Corporation
1-888-795-4274
www.Xlibris.com
Orders@Xlibris.com
83923

Contents

I could have dedicated this book to any one of the many people who have played an important role in my life. However, I chose to dedicate this book to my father, Patrick Allen Pokrandt.

Throughout our years together, he has taken the time to share with me his beliefs about determination, trust, integrity, happiness, love, commitment, humility, and success. Each day of my life, I've watched and admired him as he worked hard in order to make the lives of his children better than his own.

What is most important to me, at this moment, is that he fully understands that he has molded me through his words and his actions. I am certain that it is through those many *life lessons* he shared with me over the years, that my dad has helped to make me into the person, the husband, and the father that I have become.

Every father naturally wants his children to find the success they seek in every aspect of their lives. Thank you, Dad, for placing the road map to that success, firmly in my hand.

Acknowledgements

This collection of books would never have become a reality without these very special people in my life.

Becky Pokrandt: My wife is the one individual in this world whose life is totally committed to my success and happiness. Without her personal strength and loving commitment to endure this process of trial and error we call life, I would never have had the courage to persevere.

Courtney DeArmond: My eldest daughter is the person who first showed our family the power to be found within an individual's personal commitment to be their best. Thus, through the strength of her personality and her *never compromise* commitment to excellence, she has forever raised the bar for our entire family.

Kristine Pokrandt: My youngest daughter inspires all of us with her ability to positively influence the lives of the people around her. She shines as a beacon of light and inspiration, and the people that are drawn to her become changed for the better from the experience.

Diane Pokrandt: My mom has taught me many of the lessons seen on the pages of this book. Each of those lessons I learned were both from her words and through her examples. I love her not only because she is my mom, but also because she has always been so much more.

Ruth Taggatz: My mother-in-law has, since the day I married into her family, displayed a level of internal strength and spiritual confidence that gives each of us who know her the belief that, through faith, all things are possible.

Special Acknowledgements

Mr. John Macomber: In 1968, my sixth grade teacher, Mr. Macomber, physically stuffed me inside a locker after I called him by his first name. Through his actions, he taught me the value of respect. Not just for adults and those in charge, but more importantly for myself. His belief in me sowed the first seeds of the self-confidence, which today drives me to succeed.

Nancy Schuller: In 1984, Nancy called me to ask if I would help her to form the Eagle River Area Jaycees. Later, she nominated me to be charter president of the group. Over the years, the learning opportunities provided for me as a Jaycee, along with Nancy's support in all those efforts, changed my life.

Jay Jaehnke: In 1995, after reviewing my taxes, Jay said to me, "You are so much better than this . . . The value you bring to everything you do is so much greater." Jay was talking about how much money I made. He was right. I thank him for believing in who I was and who I could one day be. Only a true friend could dare be so honest.

Mary Jo Berner: In 1996, Mary Jo hired me away from my family business. Without having any of the limitations of traditional employer-employee relationships, she gave me the freedom to realize the potential within me to be something more. Though our business and personal relationship ended five years later, I can say that without her, I would not have found the success I now enjoy.

Eagle River, Wisconsin: Since 1983, the people in the small town where I live have made all things in my life possible. They showed me how to take responsibility for my own success, while at the same time teaching me to accept responsibility to give back more than you take. In Eagle River, people lead by example. Luckily, I've had many people whose example I could follow and whose support I still appreciate.

Foreword

My dad never intended this collection of words to be for anyone other than me, his daughter Kristine. With his permission and help, I'm choosing to share these thoughts with you now because they have been important to me. More importantly, they have had a powerful impact on my life. I am confident that there will be some idea within these pages, which, if given your due consideration, will also have the potential to change your life. That is, just as these words have powerfully changed mine.

"Success: My Thoughts on the Subject," the first book you'll find in this four-book collection was given, in part, to me on my graduation from college. I would like to share with you how, what you have in your hands, all came about. I personally think the story behind these books is special. This background will give you a colorful and meaningful context to all the ideas shared with me in each of the four books my dad gave me.

My dad told me writing the first book was really just his attempt to exert his parental influence one last time. He admits to the fact that he was unrealistically hoping that through this one last effort to be my dad, he would somehow give me leg up in my efforts to find success in life. (You know, he was right; his efforts have done just that.)

I was a business and marketing major graduating from Carthage College in Kenosha, Wisconsin. It was there, just prior to my graduation that I believe this unreasonable parental concern for my future first took root. It started with the fact that I had decided that after college I would pursue a career in sales in California. For you geography buffs, that is a long way away from where I grew up in northern Wisconsin. Yet, I can tell you that the thought of being that far from home wasn't scary to me, it was exciting! However, it seemed to sadden both my parents. The thought of my being so far away still weighs on their minds, and I've been gone for many years. Despite the distance, I know that they are proud of me. Proud of all that I have accomplished out here on my own. It is as my father's mother told him in her defending my decision to head west, "We raise our children so that they can go out into the world and make their own way," and I was most certainly going out into the world. Thanks for the support, Grandma.

Looking back, as my dad contemplated my graduation, he told me that he grew more thoughtful about what the end of my college years would mean to him. My graduation day would certainly represent a change in the lives of him and my mom. As I prepared to share my thoughts with you here, Dad took some time to explain to me how he had begun to second-guess himself as a father. How it was that he wondered if he had done all he could to give me the best possible chance for success in life. Like all parents, my mom and dad worried about how it would be for me all alone, so far from home. More than anything else, Dad shared with me his concerns about how I might survive in the *dog-eat-dog* world of sales. He had been selling his entire life, and he assured me his experience gave him reasons to worry. It's not that he was worried that I didn't have the skills, the drive, or the sensibility to succeed. But still, as he said, "It was sales."

After talking with my mom to get her perspective on all this, she believes that Dad's anxiety over this change was probably more about what he would do with himself when I was gone. You see, my sister, Courtney, had graduated from college just the year before to become a teacher like our mom. So then, the date of my graduation officially emptied the family nest. That meant after my graduation, just like after my sister's graduation, my dad could no longer see his primary role in life as Courtney and Kristy's dad. Mom said the thought of that was admittedly stressful for him to deal with.

For a decade in his life, Dad was involved in the management of radio stations. From that experience, he had come to look at effective communication in terms of thirty—and sixty-second ads. "Ideas," he often said, "all ideas had to be able to be sold in thirty to sixty seconds." His belief was that if you can learn to keep the presentation of your ideas focused, you give yourself the best chance to maintain the listener's attention. Since I was going into sales, he thought it would be a neat gift if he put his thoughts of how to be successful in sales into a number of thirty—to sixty-second ads and then format them into a book. The resulting product would be easy for him to formulate as he had been actually writing ads and training other people to sell for decades. Moreover, it would be concise enough to ensure that I would read all his thoughts. It was going to be called *60 Seconds to Selling Success*. I think that it was a great title and a great concept.

However, as the months before graduation flew by, he explained to me how he began to give into his bigger fears about my finding the greater success we all seek in life. That is, about the success we find not just between nine and five each day but the success there is to be found in the other sixteen hours each day as well.

I remember a conversation with my parents before I graduated from high school. I was telling them that I wanted to go to college at Arizona State University. The answer from the folks was pretty darn direct, "No!" Yet the reasoning behind the answer is something I'll never forget. "You are not going to Arizona to get your undergraduate degree," my dad stated. "When you graduate and go on to get your master's degree, we'll support you anywhere you want to go." He continued, "Arizona is too far away, and your mom and I still have too much parenting to do!" Still, with all that said, I knew that the decision to go or not to go to ASU was still mine to make and that my parents would support me all the way. Looking back, not going to Arizona was the right decision for me; it was the right advice for them to give me. This exchange is a good example of the kind of relationship that I have with my parents. Advice is given, a course suggested, and then they trust me to do what is best. Through it all, I certainly know that I am loved and that they are committed to my success and happiness. Dad's gift upon my graduation was just a natural extension of his instincts to provide parental guidance, showing me how much he really cared.

As my graduation deadline drew nearer and nearer, he never really let the concept of sharing with me his ideas about achieving success leave his mind. Let me try to explain. You see, my dad's greatest fear was that I had taken on more than even a much older and more experienced individual could successfully accomplish. In accepting my first job, the company who hired me did so without my having any sales experience, without my having any industry experience, and the job was in an industry where there are very few successful women. My dad insisted that the combination of factors was not generally the advice you find in an HR 101 book on the subject of successful hiring strategies. On that point, I was in full agreement. However, I was still personally confident and determined to make it all happen for myself.

My dad has been in business his entire life and has hired many people for many different types of sales jobs. He was very clear to me that he had seen many people fail under much more favorable conditions than I was walking into. He wasn't trying to kill my excitement about my future but simply to ensure I had a clear understanding of the rules of the game I was about to play. It's just that my dad had watched as people, whom he was certain had the skills and abilities to be successful, crashed and burned. Like so many other sales managers who had hired people before, he said he too often found his prediction of an employee's future success to be wrong. However, having grown up watching him deal with work, my dad didn't really need to point out to me the possible pitfalls I'd encounter as a selling professional.

As a manager, Dad never saw his people's failure as theirs alone. If they failed as salespeople, he felt that he had failed as their sales manager. He would say that he had failed to motivate, to train, to inspire, and certainly, he would feel as though he had failed to give them enough of himself to ensure their success. Given that background as the basis of his life experience, all his worries and concerns about my future certainly made sense. In the end, I know from what my mom has told me that he wondered if he similarly had failed me as well. My dad's definition of failure here is rooted in his fear that he had failed to give enough of himself to me in order to ensure my success. In our many conversations since he wrote that first book as my graduation gift, Dad has told me repeatedly that the thought of his possibly having let me down constantly haunted him.

On top of that, he was virtually certain that I would end up being let down by what he described as "some witless sales manager who would fail to realize their personal responsibility for their employee's success." Sure, I understand that employees need to take responsibility for their actions or inactions, and I expected at the time to be fully accountable for all my actions and the results of those actions. Yet he could not bear to have incompetent management end up as the fate for his daughter, especially with me being so far from home. "How could I possibly entrust her chance at long-term success to just anybody?" he said to my mom one night. I know that it was a bit melodramatic, but then being emotionally overexpressive somewhat ran in our family.

With that motivation in mind and a clear vision for his completed project, he finally started to write. For days upon days, Mom says he wrote, wrote, and rewrote. The deadline for completion of my gift was only weeks away. There, with the pressure of my graduation blowing at his back, my mom told me that he consistently stayed on task. Weekend days and every weeknight, she said he buried himself in the task. When he had finished, the result was my thirty-six-page gift. A book of advice that my dad hoped would help me to reach my goals, his shining silver bullet of advice was ready to be printed.

Well, at least he thought he was done. That is until my eighth grade English-teaching mother harshly critiqued his work for its grammar, spelling, and run-on sentences. Thank goodness, she offered to step in and help. By the way, if you find any sentences that you think are too long, they are my dad's fault, not hers. I can just see them in my mind's eye both arguing over all this. There is Mom crossing all the *t*'s, dotting all the *i*'s, and cropping short all the run-on sentences. Dad, he is there arguing against every change. The thought of how I imagine those conversations went, well, it all just makes me smile.

Like all authors, at least famous ones, Dad had boldly entered his name on the cover of his finished work, written *by Perry Pokrandt*. Mom told me the story about how, after my dad e-mailed my gift to the printer, he looked relieved. She laughed when she told me how proud he was of himself. "It was written all over his face," she said. I can tell you that he clearly has the right to feel proud of his effort. Yet even though it felt good to be done, he told her that in the back of his mind, he wasn't really sure about something. Of course, he said he was confident about the ideas he had written down for me to consider. Mom told me that Dad loved the book's title. It was "unassuming," he said. Dad was certain that "Success: My Thoughts on the Subject" would have an impact on me, and he was pleased that he had finished it all on time. Yet despite all the positive feelings, he continued to be uneasy. As he tells the story, "I just couldn't get over my feeling that something wasn't right." Maybe it was just nerves, you know, his wondering how I would receive his labor of love on graduation day. Trying to ease his doubts, he scanned the pages of his book, looking for what he felt was missing. (My dad's behavior is often said to be a bit obsessive-compulsive.) Then as this story goes, he saw it—*by Perry Pokrandt.* I loved it the first time he shared this part of the story with me. "There it was, front and center, *by Perry Pokrandt.*" As he explained to me, in his mind, Perry Pokrandt wasn't the one who wrote this book. He believes that only Kristine's dad could have found the motivation to record the thoughts you will read here. Motivation based upon his worry, hope, and fear. With that realization, he made the simple correction to the cover by deleting his name and typing in how I've always known him, as my dad, *Kristine's dad.* Now it was official. Kristine's dad was the author. As Dad tells it, Perry alone could never have taken on this project. That's because Perry would never have been able to find the words. However, I want you to know my dad did—Kristine's dad did.

The Wednesday before my graduation, he finally picked up his gift to me at the printer. It was, he hoped, just a little something extra to protect his little girl from the big bad world. I know that is also somewhat melodramatic as well, I warned you. However, that's how he described to me how he felt. When he got the book in his hands for the first time, he admits to feeling overwhelmed. The woman from the print shop, who had provided him so much help in its printing, told him what a wonderful gift he had created. She said how much she and her coworkers had enjoyed actually reading his gift to me. "You really should get this published," she told him. "I just did!" he responded.

When I look back to the weeks before my graduation, I unknowingly helped my dad with this project, as each day he'd call me and read a few of the writings you will find on the pages here. He told me he was just preparing for a sales meeting, and he was looking for some feedback on the specific topics he was going to cover. Each of these pages, he said, represented one of the pieces of advice he planned to share during that training session. Little did I know he was using that story to gauge my reaction and feed off my insight. He just wanted to get a feel as to how I would receive his thoughts when I opened his gift.

I'm certain now, that it was those pregraduation talks that were the best gift of all. Here I was, yet to graduate, and my dad was asking me for input on so many different aspects of how to help his people achieve success in sales. Training a person to sell, that's something he'd been doing his entire life, and he was asking for my insight. I think that it was somewhere in one of those many conversations that my dad decided to change the focus of my gift from his goals to help me to achieve selling success, to the higher goal of helping me achieve a greater level of success in life. As you read many of the pages, you could easily insert the word *selling* somewhere into the text without having the advice be the least bit off course.

When he gave me my book on the day of my graduation, I cried a little, and we all laughed a lot. Quickly after opening, I tucked the gift away. I was, at that moment, content to finish opening my other gifts and save my dad's words for a later time. That is, I was content to wait for a time when I could be alone and have a chance to reflect on all the thoughts you will now also get to read.

My reaction later that day is not as important at this point as your own will be. Suffice it to say, that to this day, I carry that book and all the other books he has given me wherever I go. When it's been a rough day or challenges seem overwhelming, my dad is always there to support me within the pages of my books, just as he has always been there for me while growing up. In these moments, I randomly open one of the books, taking a few minutes to read a few pages. There in the words on each page, I see my dad. I feel his love, and I know that he is with me. Take these words with you as I have done and use them as I do in order to chart a road map for your own success.

During my first year out of college, I sure did come up against it, just as Dad had feared. It seemed as though each and every day brought new challenges; I guess that's life. Most were challenges that my mom and dad could not really help me solve. I think I was driving my parents nuts with the novel-like life I was living. In order to calm his stress, Mom says that Dad just kept writing. She didn't know who he thought he was writing for; perhaps he was hoping that somewhere in those additional thoughts, he could help me to find my path. He just wanted to help me chart my course forward, to help me find myself.

By the time Christmas had come at the end of my graduation year, he had finished what was the second half of that first book, "Success: My Thoughts on the Subject." What he started and thought he had finished when he gave it to me as a graduation gift only months before, now was truly done with seventy total entries.

During this time, life on the coast did not settle down. Shortly after the holiday season, the relationship with the first company that had hired me out of college started to go south. You see, the owner of the company started to walk away from many of the promises made both to me and to my father. It was just as my dad had warned, just as he had feared. However, each day, through it all, my parents were there for me. Together we all lived through the ups and downs as they worked with me to help guide me through each of the challenges that I faced.

All during that time, my dad, though I only found this out later, kept writing. He says now that his writing may have been more about making him feel valuable than it was really about helping me to survive California. He had no plans to put his thoughts together into a second book. Nevertheless, upon the first anniversary of my graduation, my dad surprised me again by presenting me with his second book, "Next Level: More Thoughts on the Subject of Success."

Now Dad says that it was really somewhere in the process of writing the thoughts that are now part of that second book that he began to realize the power of the ideas that he had shared with me. It seemed as though once or twice a week, I would call to tell him how something I had read in his book had helped me to deal with a specific situation. It was then and still is a marvelous tool for me.

During the next year and a half, Dad said that he had continued to record random thoughts as they came to him. Sometimes he would call me, excited about what he had just written as he wanted to share the thought with me right then and there. He kept insisting that he never really planned for anything to come from those ideas as that was why he was reading them to me over the phone. It was now kind of like a hobby, some dads play golf, some dads tinker with old cars, and my dad writes stuff. He had written two books, and he felt like he was and should be done.

I had gotten a new job with DHL as a freight consolidation specialist. I was pretty darn good at it too, even if I do say so myself. Everything was going so well at that time, that is until DHL dissolved its US freight operation. Again, my world turned upside down. However, this time, my mom was battling cancer, and our family was in the midst of planning my sister's wedding. It seems that there just wasn't time to give much thought to my situation. It looked and felt like it was all up to me now. Talk about feeling alone and far from home.

It was when I came home for my sister's wedding in June of 2009, in talking to me face-to-face, my parents realized how hard it had been during those long months of DHL's demise. My parents joked that worrying about me had almost become their second job. Yet both my parents said that the idea of a third book had not been talked about until after the trip my dad took to visit me in San Diego a few months after the wedding.

Dad can be a bit of a nut, and positive proof of that fact is in the story he told me about the night before he flew to San Diego to visit me in October of 2009. He said that he virtually could not sleep that night in his motel room as so many ideas were buzzing in his head. With his creative juices flowing, he got out of bed and he wrote. He wrote for hours, only by the light of his BlackBerry. (Crazy, I know!) In all, he finished twenty of the thoughts that you will find in his third book. He describes the burst of creativity as if the gates of emotion had reopened after the stress of the wedding, and my mom's illness had subsided. As I said, during that prewedding time, my mom also dealt with cancer, and as you can imagine, that time was more than a bit stressful. For those many months, my parents had more than enough on their plate; they didn't need to also be worrying about me.

As my dad looks back, he thinks that perhaps that burst of creative energy was triggered by his excitement and anticipation about the two of us getting to spend time together. It had been over a year and a half since he had given me that second book, and he obviously still had so many things he wanted to say. Now he felt it was time to share. With those twenty thoughts he had written that night, plus the ones he wrote on the next day's flight out to San Diego, plus the ones he'd already written at home over those many months, he now had about forty written. That was more than half as many as he needed for a third book. However, it wasn't until he and I went hiking in Torrey Pines State Natural Reserve, his first day in San Diego, that the focus of that third book came clear to him.

When my dad arrived home that next week, he had a clear goal in mind: he would finish the third book and give it to me by the third anniversary of my college graduation. "View from the Top: My Final Thoughts on the Subject of Success" was the result of that visit. By early February, that third book was done months before the May deadline. Well, at least, he had written the rough drafts of the seventy thoughts the book would contain. Now he needed to wait for my mom to edit them.

This time, the editing took a bit longer than planned. As my mom will tell you or anyone else who might listen, she has a life outside her role as editor for my dad. Dad missed that third anniversary date by a few months. But during that time, while reading a copy of Glenn Beck's *Arguing with Idiots*, Dad envisioned the final piece of the puzzle, a fourth book, "King of the Hill: How to Stay a Success Once You Become One." He hadn't even given me the third book yet, and he was off and writing again on the fourth.

He says that the last book all came together while he and mom were on vacation in Mexico with my sister Courtney and me in March of 2010. He wrote all week long, though I'm not sure any of us noticed between those umbrella drinks as we enjoyed the sun. As he tells it, while we shared time together on the beach, he was able to see clearly so many of the lessons that he had learned throughout his life with all of us. Perhaps in many ways, this last, very last, of the literary gifts from my dad is the most special. The reason is that I know we were all together as a family when he wrote each word.

My dad signed my first book and all my books with; "*You inspire me to be better than I really am.*" He based his words upon the story of our family. It is founded upon the influence we've all had on each other's lives. My dad says that he doesn't know who he would be today without my mom, Becky, in his life. I know that he has always aspired to be better than he really is in order to justify her love for him. He tells the story that he aspired to be better than he really was from the very moment his first daughter was born as he could never bear the thought of letting her down. I was the last of the line. But of course, never the least, and with three women in his life to keep driving him forward, the inscription seemed just so right.

When he wrote those words at that time, I don't know if he truly understood how clearly they reflected each of us as a part of him. Nothing else he could have possibly written could have been more powerful and moving. I believe that each of us in the family is who we are because of how we motivate each other to be our best. My sister Courtney motivated me academically and musically while at the same time, I challenged her socially and athletically. My sister and I motivated each other to be better than we really are, and I, for one, am grateful. We constantly challenged each other to be what we jokingly refer to as *overachievers.* In our family, to be considered an overachiever is the greatest of compliments, and I'm proud to be considered one myself.

As kids, my sister and I set our own standards, and my mom and dad strived to be role models in order to not let us down. They didn't always succeed. Yet, I'm certain that we are who we are because each of them always aspired to be better than they really were. For good or bad, we all individually raised the bar for each other, and I think that things seemed to have worked out pretty well because of that.

So then, why is it so important that I share this book, or should I say these books, with you? Well, as my dad's writing went on, he said that it became as much about him helping himself as it was about him helping me. As I understand it, his writing helped him to redefine for himself the important lessons that he thought critical to finding the success we all seek from life, and that included him. I'm pretty certain that your experience has taught you many of the same lessons my dad's experiences have taught him. I imagine that like my dad and me, you too will benefit from his introspective revelations. Enjoy your journey of rediscovery as you are reminded of many of your own life lessons.

Seriously, I know now more than ever that much of what he's written here has the power to change a life. That is because his words have changed mine. We all have a responsibility to pay those positive things in our lives forward, and my dad charged me with the responsibility to share with others what he's shared with me. So now, working with his permission, I share this with you. Not because I know or believe that you need to change your life. I share these ideas because I know the positive impact that they have had on my own life, and I want that for you as well.

These gifts to me, I now see as my gift to you. But like any opportunity, it's what we do with it that makes the difference. I know this because the words my dad has written have no power in and of themselves. Yet it is important that you know and understand that these words have empowered me in situations where, without their guidance, I am certain I would have fallen short. I think it is because I have taken my father's advice to heart that these books have allowed me to find myself or see my future on every page.

I hope you will also find a key to the additional success you've been searching for within the pages of this book. So again, please accept this gift from my father and me in the spirit of respect and admiration in which it is offered. Decide for yourself if that woman from the print shop, who helped my dad with his graduation gift to me, was right in her recommendation to him—*"You really should get this published."* I certainly hope you'll agree!

One last thing before you turn the next few pages and begin reading "Success," the first of my dad's books. I'd like to extend to you an invitation. Even though you and I may not know each other, after you have read my dad's words within these pages, I'm certain that you will then feel as though you do know him. So let me say that I'd very much appreciate, when you have finished this book, that you take a minute to share your thoughts about what you have read directly with my father. Let him know what you really think about this collection of ideas about achieving success. Good or bad, I ask you to consider sharing your feelings from your perspective as a boss, employee, student, parent, or as a friend. Tell him if his words have touched you in any way. Let him know if what he has written reminded you of the road you have traveled or triggered a memory that even made you laugh. I know that he would even want you to be honest about which of his ideas you totally believe to be wrong. Write or e-mail him if these ideas confirmed something you also personally believe to be true or if his words inspired you as they have me.

—Kristine Pokrandt

Please share your impressions with him as your feedback will in turn be my gift to him.

You can reach him directly
via e-mail at
perrypokrandt@sharelifelessons.com
by US mail at
Perry Pokrandt, 4887 Echo Ridge Drive
Eagle River, WI 54521

(I promise you, he will be glad to hear from you.)

Letter to Dad

Author's note:

When my daughter Kristine first suggested that she wanted to get her books, a gift from me, published, I balked at the idea. That is until she shared with me this letter expressing how my words had influenced her life. After reading how what I had written for her had personally affected her, I changed my mind and gave her my permission, with one condition. I insisted that her letter to me be included within the final product. Against her initial protests, she agreed to share her letter with you. The reason that I felt it important that her thoughts be included here is to help each of you clearly understand what these words have meant to her. More importantly, I felt that her thoughts would help you to believe in all the possibilities the journey ahead could hold for you.

9/1/2010

Dear Dad,

Since my graduation from college, on countless occasions, I have had the chance to share our story one-on-one with friends, business associates, and customers. I use it as an opportunity for them to know me better through the things I believe as written in your books. My request for you to allow me to get your thoughts published is my chance to bring these ideas to as many people as possible. Doing so would be my opportunity to share with everyone what your words have meant to me. Getting these books published is our chance to tell the entire world the story behind the little spiral-bound books I carry with me every day. This letter represents the official culmination of this part of our journey, and it is my way of thanking you for all you have done for me.

A number of years back when I took my first job in Arizona, I had big dreams and was filled with the greatest sense of optimism possible. As you know, I have always had the fighting spirit within me that allows me to push past obstacles. You've seen firsthand how driven I can be in my daily efforts to prove the skeptics wrong. The challenge of my first job was no different. In the face of the doubt and concern surrounding my decision to go to Phoenix, I intended to prove to all that what I was attempting to achieve was more than just possible but that I would excel in my efforts.

As that first year in my new job had passed, what I had accomplished by growing my territory by 300 percent with no sales background or industry experience was a great source of personal pride. For me, exceeding those goals was a bigger victory than winning any MVP athletic award, more humbling than earning my full-ride scholarship to Carthage College, and more gratifying than being selected to give the commencement speech at both my high school and college graduations. The positive emotional impact of that first success on me was even greater than the uplifting emotions I experienced the summer I volunteered on the Gulf Coast after Hurricane Katrina. That first year was filled with so much emotion.

As you know, my story is much more complicated than what I can share here in the pages of this letter to you. As of this moment, I have now been here in California over three years. A lot has changed in my life as I am now three jobs, four apartments, and one broken heart stronger. Yet, the many dark days have failed to cast a shadow on the fact that I have also been blessed with great friends, a career that allows me to grow, and a life I am truly proud of. The true success story for me is that, through it all and against the odds, I have created a really good life for myself.

As you remember, most of that first year in my first job I actually was in California. Things changed fast as my company had moved me from Phoenix just a month into my new job. So much for my putting down roots in the desert! As it turned out, I realized after all the glitz and the glam of California living started to fade, it had all become very real. You had been right; I was up against a very large hurdle. As you said, I was just twenty-two, still had very little industry experience, was a female in a very much male-dominated sales market, and I was alone.

One day, about a month into my California adventure, I was going through the stuff in the trunk of my car, as some like to call it, my mobile closet. There amongst my trunk treasures was your graduation gift, my little spiral-bound book. I grabbed it, pulled it to the front seat with me, and flipped to the first entry. I read just two short paragraphs, yet from that moment on, those words would change my life.

Those who claim it can't be done are left to try to draw their satisfaction from what can best be called their nonaccomplishment.

Those who believe it can be done may fail in their effort, but no one can ever say they failed to strive. It is in the process of striving, in the very struggle itself, that the seeds for an individual's success are sown.

These words resonated in me. I could hear those people around me who had said I was making a mistake, who told me that the odds were against me, who said right out loud that I would not succeed. I was not going to let any of them be right!

As you know, it gets lonely when selling on the road. There you are, faced with challenge after challenge, all alone with little or no real support. However, as I would occasionally feel my spirits sink, you were there to help me regroup. Throughout each day, I would pause for a minute and open a page of my book, my gift from you. As I read, I could literally hear your voice. It was as if you were there speaking to me. I could go on and on about how each entry in this compilation of your books has affected me, but my coffee cup is empty now, so here is where I will end. However, before I go, just one last thought to be shared between us.

I know you remember back in 2000 when the movie Castaway, starring Tom Hanks, came out. It was a story about a man marooned all alone on an island, except for a volleyball he creatively had named Wilson. As odd as that may sound outside the context of the movie's script, Wilson became Tom Hanks's character's best and only friend. Wilson was his sole confidante, his pride, and his joy and the lone thread linking him to any degree of his sanity. The point is, Dad, that many times during this great adventure I am on, I have also found myself feeling like I too am alone on an island, an island that is far, far from home.

The very point of this letter to you is to ensure that you know these books and the conversations we were able to have—because of them—were my "Wilson." What I am trying to say here is that your words saved me. They saved me in every sense of the word. They motivated and pushed me, at times they held my hand, and at times, they were the very thing that dried my tears. Your words in these books forced me to think in new ways, allowed me truly to love, and encouraged me to reach. The thoughts contained here were the voice that assured me each day how great I could really be.

I believe that you have known all along how your words have become a part of my journey and how they influence me on a daily basis. Nevertheless, this letter to you is the first time I have ever attempted to put my thoughts and feelings about this entire process onto paper.

What started out as your words of advice became my words to live by, they inspired many ideas of my own, and they became part of who I am and how I endeavor to live my life. If in the beginning your intention was, as you've said, to make one last attempt to save me from this big bad world, then know for certain that your intent was fully realized. Dad, your words did save me. Also know that the true result of all your efforts has been that you've allowed me to truly find myself; as three years and four books later, I feel as though I have finally arrived.

I believe the greatest gift that these books have given both of us is that those spiral-bound pages now tell our story. It is the story of how our very normal father-and-daughter relationship forever changed into an extraordinary bond that is irreplaceable and one that is beyond my words.

I love you,

Kristine

First Words

"Now, have you finally learned your lesson?" I heard these words said after being sent to my room for snitching some cookies and then not eating my dinner. That was just after being told, "Eating cookies now will spoil your appetite."

"Good, maybe now you'll have learned your lesson!" I heard these words said after losing the money my parents gave me to go to the fair. That was just after being told, "Put that money in your wallet. If you just stuff it in your pants pocket, you'll lose it."

"So did you finally learn your lesson?" I heard these words said after firecrackers exploded in my hand. That was just after being told, "Don't play with fireworks. They're dangerous, and you could get hurt."

"I certainly hope that you've learned your lesson!" I heard these words said after losing my driver's license just weeks before the junior prom for driving twenty miles per hour over the speed limit in a school zone. That was just after being told, "You can have the car, but please drive safely."

"Now that you've learned your lesson, maybe you'll listen to me next time!" I heard these words said the morning I woke up with a hangover after drinking too much the night before. That was just after being told, "You know, if you drink too much, you're going to get sick."

"Well, I hope this has taught you a lesson!" Throughout my entire life, even after my becoming an adult, people have expressed this sentiment after seemingly every mistake I made.

The book you are about to read contains the many lessons that life has taught me along the road to where I am today. I have learned lessons from my mistakes, and I have learned lessons from the times I was lucky enough to get it right the first time.

Though I wrote down this collection of *life lessons*, I cannot take credit for them. Each of these lessons has been taught to me by my grandparents, parents, and wife, as well as by our children, family members, friends, and by my coworkers.

Prior to taking on the challenge of sharing the lessons my life's experiences have taught me, I had no concept of how many times it sometimes took me actually to learn my lesson. Evidently, in retrospect, I might not have been quite as sharp as I thought at the time. If I had been, the road I have been on might have been a whole lot smoother. Often, I joke that I have learned all my lessons the hard way. However, at the time, that process didn't always seem quite so funny.

It is these life lessons that are now the basis of my title for this compilation of four books given first to my daughter Kristine. Each of these books are filled with my thoughts about achieving success, and each entry came out of the hard-learned lessons life has provided me. The fact is you do not have to be like me. That is, learning each of your lessons the hard way. By reading these books, you can benefit from my experience by judging the value of my lessons learned for yourself.

This introspective, retrospective process has had value for my daughter and me. I hope that the result you hold in your hands, "Life Lessons: What Experience Teaches Us About Success," will have value to you as well. It's important to me that you realize after having turned that last page, that like me, you too have learned from my lessons.

Success

My Thoughts on the Subject

by Kristine's dad

Dear Kristine,

As you move away from our home in order to make a home of your own, my opportunities to shape your life through the lessons I have learned will be rare. Our conversations will be less frequent, and your struggle and vulnerability will be easier to hide behind the speaker of the phone. I think with the physical distance that will be between us, you will probably find it easy to avoid your dad's next lecture on how you should better live your life.

As I sit here, I am afraid that so many of the lessons I have yet to share with you will go unshared. I am even more afraid that the lessons I have had the opportunity to share with you will be lost or forgotten. So as my gift to you, I have recorded in writing those things that I believe could be keys to finding success in your life. I hope as you read them, you too will find many of these thoughts to have meaning, helping you find purpose and find your way. It is from within this collection of ideas that I also hope you can gain a greater understanding of the important lessons that have made me into the person you have always known.

As I first started writing down this advice, I could not help but think about what this book would be like if your mother were to have written it with me. Her words would be so different from mine. You know, it is our differences that make me love her so much. I see so much of your mom in you. I wish I could say that thought always makes me smile, but sometimes it only makes me shake my head. Yet together, what she and I have been able to give to you is in total what makes up the two halves of the whole that you have become. You are who you are not because everything your mom and I ever told you was agreed upon. You are who are specifically because it was not. That makes me wonder if two wrongs can really make a right. Because, Kristy, you absolutely are so right as a person. Your mother and I have both shared with you so many of the things that we believe you need to know. Yet I am sure many times you've wondered to yourself how it is that two so opposite views of the world can both possibly be right. Well, I do not know the answer to that for certain, but I am pretty sure there is more than one right answer to many of life's mysteries.

That's why with so many different, powerful, and successful philosophies of how to live your life, you will most certainly find yourself, from time to time, receiving conflicting advice on how to succeed from equally successful people. The confusion will at times be overwhelming as you struggle to do the right thing. Nevertheless, I know you will work to figure out what is best for you.

I also know that you have set goals for yourself, and because of that, I am very proud of you. I think that a logical, well-grounded person probably believes that there has to be a single best way to reach one's goals. However, just as there are two ways around to the other side of a tree, life provides us many equally rewarding ways to reach our goals. Yet as I write down my thoughts on the subject of finding success, I really do have to wonder how it is that two conflicting ideas can possibly both end up being the right answer.

I know that you understand the ethical concept of taking the high road. You really have to wonder what that really means. Is there really a perfectly clear definition of right and wrong? Well, on some level I hope there is. I know that as your parents, your mom and I taught you that there is a clear difference. Yet is there really? The problem for us, as individuals, comes in what we find at the edges of the definition of words like *right* and *wrong*, *high road* and *low road*, *success* and *failure*, or *black* and *white*. How can individuals possibly find a black-and-white road map to success when each day all of life's conflicting shades of grey confront them?

In this gift to you, I have written down what I believe to be some of the best lessons taught to me and shared with me by those who cared about my success. It is a road map to success of sorts, though certainly not a black and white one. As you take in these words of so-called wisdom, you may be struck by the fact that what I say at one time may seem to be somewhat contradicted by me just a few pages later. No different than growing up at home, I say. The challenge is still in defining or deciding for yourself what is right for you. No, the answers in life will not come in black and white or right and wrong. However, answers will come to us through thoughtful consideration and commitment to the process of learning. We need to know and understand who it is we are and be able to define who we want to be. We do all this based, in the end, on what we believe to be true.

How is it that two statements of seemingly opposite orientation can both be thought of as equally true? I really do not know the answer to that. Nevertheless, what I do know is that all of what you will read here has, at one time or another, been good advice for me. Maybe, as you read the words on a certain page, they will reach out and speak to you. Then again, maybe you will find some advice where your first response is just to shake your head, either in disbelief or in confusion about what I was really trying to say to you. You'd think that since I put together these thoughts to share with you, that I should be more certain that I am directing you down the right path, sending you off on the high road, or pushing you toward the fast track. At one time or another, I can tell you that I have taken all these words to heart. Yet even as I write and edit them, I find my emotional response to each change every time I reread them.

With that being said, my first words of advice to help you solve this dilemma of what is right for you is to suggest that you read these words more than once. Maybe you should read them even more than twice. I suggest that from time to time, you just grab this collection of thoughts and take a moment to reread a few. I wrote them in single-page simplicity for just that purpose. It is important to me that you can, without effort, take a second look at these thoughts. I want you to look at these words over time. Then as you continue to grow as a person, your experiences will give you new insights into what these words may have meant to my mentors, what they may have meant to me, and what they actually now mean to you.

Some of these thoughts will hit you like a *ton of bricks*, while others will pass by almost unnoticed as you read them. Sometimes, the words will reach deep into your heart, while at other times, all you will be seeing on a page is a collection of letters forming a collection of words, and you will not feel connected to those words at all. These pages are filled with what I believe are thoughts worthy of your consideration; perhaps not all of them are equally worthy. But as I wrote them all down, I felt that each and every word played a role in relating to you specific ideas on how to be more successful in life. So take from these pages those ideas that fit who you are today and take from these pages those ideas that will help you define who you want to be tomorrow.

When confronted in life by what seems to be conflicting advice, just remember your mom and your dad arguing about whether or not you should get your ears pierced, stay out past midnight, drop Spanish class, or . . . well, you get the idea. Sometimes you will be able to see clearly the road you should travel. While at other times, you will be required to measure each of your steps against the stones along a seldom-traveled path. Whether you decide this time to walk boldly forward along the clearly marked road or you choose to tread lightly as you pick your way, it matters not as the choice is yours. All that matters is your commitment to follow it through to the end you desire.

So go forward from here as if you are turning a page in your life, because you are. I hope that you find that within my gift, as in life, there is a lot for you to discover.

Love always,

Dad

Contents: Success

#1 ~ Can't Be Done

Those who claim that something *cannot be done* are left to draw their satisfaction from what they can best refer to as their lifetime of *nonaccomplishment.*

Those who believe it *can be done* may fail in their effort, but no one can ever say that they failed to strive. It is in this process of striving, in the very struggle itself, that the seeds are sown for an individual's future success.

I have heard it said that, "To live and not to love is never to have lived." I believe that is what taking risks is all about. If that is so, then you must realize the greatest risk you will take will more likely be found in your personally choosing to not take the chance at all.

So go out. Take the risk!

Prove to everyone; prove to yourself that it really can be done, and that you are the person to do it!

I promise, when you set your fears aside and take the risk, you will find glorious satisfaction in your accomplishment of that which was thought not to be possible.

#2 ~ Sink or Swim

When thrown into the working world, no one gives you water wings to help you keep your head above water. It is only through your instinctual will to survive that you find for yourself the opportunity to succeed.

Life does not come with training wheels. It just expects you to hop on and start pedaling. I guess that is the secret to success . . . Never stop pedaling!

You truly have a chance to realize success when you play an active role in searching out life's most important lessons. That is what I mean when I tell you to take responsibility for your own journey.

When your parents first took the training wheels off your bike, they gave you a push and just let go. In that moment, you had few choices. My memory says they were simply to fail or to succeed. It was crash and burn, or you could just keep pedaling.

If your parents had never let go of you or your bike, there never would have been the need for you to make that choice. Sure, it is great to have a safety net when you go out into the world. However, with no risk to drive your actions, you always will wonder how hard you might have pedaled and how far you would have gone all on your own.

#3 ~ Best Teacher

Without the opportunity and ability to learn from our mistakes, we would find the accomplishment of our goals even more elusive.

They say that failure is the best teacher of the lessons on how we should act in order to achieve success. However, it is not simply failure itself that lights our way to our future success. It is our determination to draw enlightenment from each opportunity life gives us to fail.

Failure to take each opportunity and learn from its result can only lead us to make the same mistakes again and again.

This type of relentless futility is not really a preferred option. Rather, you should decide to take on the challenge of making the necessary changes in your life. Then use what you have learned from your failures to get to where you want to go.

Within this process of enlightenment, you will find the power to go forward. More importantly, with this knowledge you will now have the ability to achieve a different result.

#4 ~ Judge Not

What of life is so trivial that is not worth learning more about it? Then, armed with that additional information, you can draw your own conclusions. Be careful though, as many people with good intentions, like me, will tell you what it is they think they know. It is not to say their knowledge has little or no value or that you should not take the time to listen to what their experience has taught them. But, and it's a big but, they are not you. Therefore, it should be no surprise that their thoughts and the lessons they may have learned through their experience could be different from your own. It is all because the personal experiences upon which they draw are certainly not the same as yours.

So take the time to see all of life for yourself. Only then should you draw conclusions, your own conclusions, regarding how it is you really see the world around you.

As a rule, you should never fail to take the time to listen with an open mind to those who wish to share what their experience has taught them. When you do, perhaps then the most unexpected of things will happen to you. That is, all those people, and the lessons they have learned through their own unique experiences, will show you new ways to see what your own experience may have failed to clearly reveal. Thus, by having an open mind, you potentially will be enlightened!

#5 ~ Keep the Fire Burning

Burnout is simply a temporary loss of sufficient fuel to feed your life's burning passion. It is not, as often portrayed, the final flicker of your passion's last ember.

What then does it take to relight the fire within a person who believes they can no longer compete because they feel burned out?

Think first of a campfire. You have the logs, the smaller sticks, and the fine flammables. It is not collecting the necessary elements that creates the roaring fire. As any good camper knows, to have a successful fire, you must place each element purposefully within the fire ring. No one element makes the difference. The camper finds their success within the step-by-step process that allows them to build their fire.

Should you ever need to restart passion's fire within you, I suggest you clear away the clutter and remove the burden of life's bigger logs. Only when you take off the tangle of twigs and get back to the simplicity of the basics can you breathe life back into a dying flame.

In order to rebuild the fire within you, start with the elements of your life that bring you the most enjoyment. Next, add in the elements that bring you the fastest rewards. Then use your newly generated desire to burn the logs of real accomplishment and joy.

#6 ~ You Should Listen

If a tree falls in the woods, and no one is around to hear it, does it make a sound? It is more than an interesting thought to ponder. The idea can actually have a lot to do with your ultimate success in life. Maybe, just as importantly, it can have a lot to do with what could be your lack thereof.

Every day, trees are falling all around you. The question is, "Are you listening?"

In real life, the trees I am talking about in this metaphor are the needs and wants of those individuals upon whom you depend to reach your goals. The trees, so to speak, are the people around you who you work with and live with. These individuals can be either part of your life's problems or they are part of those solutions that support your own efforts to reach your goals.

As the trees fall, they may be asking you for just a bit of respect. As the trees around you fall, they may be looking for you to lend them a helping hand. As the trees fall, they may be only looking for a sympathetic ear. You need the trees, and you will find that they will only hear you when you have taken the time to listen to them.

Don't turn a deaf ear to the people around you, or you'll find the trees actually do fall silently within the forest.

#7 ~ Little Red Hen Psychology

Who will help me sow the wheat?

Who will help me bake the bread?

Despite the Little Red Hen's best efforts to enlist the help of those around her, she found no one willing to make an effort to help in reaching the mutually beneficial reward of the *fresh bread.*

What the Little Red Hen understood was the necessity in life to actually do the work before expecting to enjoy the reward.

That is how it is with successful people as well. You will not see truly successful people looking for the reward before putting in the effort necessary to achieve that desired result.

The prize is never awarded at the beginning of the contest. So go out, work hard, and then watch as the rewards for your effort will never stop coming.

#8 ~ Cutting Corners

In the book, *Little Red Riding Hood,* we all know that the wolf got to Grandma's house ahead of Red by taking the shortcut.

"My, Grandma, what big white teeth you have!" Little Red Riding Hood exclaimed.

The problem here is that, from a young age, each of us was taught that the game of life could be won by taking shortcuts. We arrive as an adult with a clear understanding of the advantages gained just by our finding a shortcut to our goal. Yet it is due to this mistaken belief in the magic of shortcuts that many of us still struggle in our search for success. That is because we believe that there must always be an easier way, and we find ourselves lost when we fail to find it.

One day, when you are older, someone will ask you, "What has been the key to your success?" The answer you will give, where you credit your focus, hard work, commitment, and personal investment, will likely fall on deaf ears. That is because none of those reasons represents what anyone would consider as a shortcut. Your answer to their questions will not be heard. That is because people do not want to hear your truth. Some people desperately need to believe that there is always a shortcut, an easier way.

Yet, I want to assure you that even though the wolf may have known a shorter way, in real life, you only achieve success through your willingness to travel every step along its long, hard road.

#9 ~ Failure is Not an Option

There is little more that needs to be said regarding your journey to be successful other than to tell you that *failure is not an option.*

If you ever find yourself hanging by a branch off the side of a very steep cliff, I hope you will understand that failure, represented by letting go of the branch, is not an option.

However, too often we do let go, having been fooled into giving up just when success is at hand. Too often, we fool ourselves into believing that whatever the ending result, it will probably be good enough. Too often, we fool ourselves into believing that even though we have not reached our goal, what we have done is our best.

The terrible thing is that in each of these cases, we will find that we are only fooling ourselves. You need to remember that failure can never be an option when, in the end, your goal is to succeed.

#10 ~ BINGO

"B~3 . . ."

"Bingo!" you yell. "I win, I win!"

As much fun as it is, life is not very much like the game of bingo. In life, success seldom is won by those who sit back with their daubers at the ready just waiting around for their number to be called.

In life, if you want to win the game, it is up to you to seek out and find your own B~3. It is up to you to get those things for yourself that you will need in order to be successful. You will find no victory is possible while you are sitting back and waiting for the game to come to you.

Sure, when you play the game of bingo, someone always wins. My point however, is that everybody does not win at bingo. Just one person wins, maybe two if there is a tie. The truth is simple: in bingo, the majority of players lose in every game!

You cannot afford to play the game of life as people play the game of bingo. If you did, the odds of success would then be stacked against you every day. Stop sitting back, just waiting around until someone else calls your winning number. Take this lesson, go out there, and give life a spin. Then reach out and grab your own success from inside the spinning tumbler.

#11 - Do it Again and Again

Skills, in life, are developed through repetition, whereas luck is a one-and-done thing!

I say, either "you *get* lucky, or you *become* successful." The difference is in your commitment to the development of the skills you need in order to consistently be successful.

I have heard it described that Tiger Woods practices thousands of four-foot putts from a single spot. Repetition of that nature develops the consistency that allows Tiger the confidence necessary to win.

Repetition, consistency, confidence, success . . .
Repetition, consistency, confidence, success . . .
Repetition, consistency, confidence, success . . .

It is Tiger's prior success, gained through consistent preparation, which gives him his unshaken confidence. It is this kind of repetitive preparation for a successful outcome that has the power to silence the self-doubt that resides within all of us, including Tiger Woods.

When you have prepared for success and that preparation has resulted in your achieving the success you prepared for, it is easy to understand how the mind becomes conditioned to only allow you to visualize your success when presented with that challenge.

Would you rather rely on the skills you have worked to develop or hope to be lucky enough to make the putt?

#12 ~ A Pendulum Swings Both Ways

Why do so many things about a person's life seem to remain the same? The answer—*fear of change!*

Why do some people always seem to be evolving, growing, succeeding? The answer—*desire for change!*

In dealing with people, we can almost divide the world into these two distinctive parts: one part fears the unknown, while the second part lives for it, pursues it, and cherishes every chance to experience it.

Which way does your pendulum swing?

I am not suggesting that a bit of stability in one's life is a bad thing. However, I can tell you that you will find a high level of tolerance for change more often in people who are afraid of only one thing, and that is that the world will pass them by if they do not change with it.

The one thing you must understand about the challenge ahead is that, with all the things in your life that have helped you get to where you are today, the status quo will not be sufficient to keep you there. The world around you is changing constantly in direct opposition to our best efforts to maintain the comfort of your personal status quo.

Change is inevitable, like it or not. Yet, I believe success too is inevitable once you have learned to manage that change.

#13 ~ No Advantage in Tomorrow

Start when you have a dream, start when you have a goal, start when you have a plan . . . *Start today!*

There are very few instances where you will gain an advantage by waiting until tomorrow, that will be sufficient to offset the momentum gained by your decision to start today.

Success is elusive enough without postponing your efforts to achieve it. Maybe the most powerful argument for today is that for many people, the tomorrow they hope for never arrives. If they are not careful, life just has a way of getting in the way. When life gets in the way, those people who didn't start today will find that much-anticipated first day of the rest of their lives will always be seen as tomorrow.

So go ahead and draw your line in the sand. Make today the day when you put your plan in action. Make today the day when you begin the chase for your dreams.

#14 ~ Lesson of the Golden Arches

What is it about McDonald's that makes them McDonald's? I submit to you that it is not the unequaled quality of the food they serve. Though, it is certainly true that people agree with the fact that their fries are pretty darn good. Let me suggest that their success comes not from the fact that their fries are pretty darn good, but that their fries are pretty darn good every time!

McDonald's and their unequaled success defines for us the value of consistency in the achievement of your goals.

In sports, everyone has heard of an athlete described as *being in a zone.* We reserve these words of praise for a competitor who is performing with incredible consistency. The admiration found in that statement does not just define that person's level of excellence, but it more importantly defines the consistency of their excellent performance.

Are you in a zone when dealing with the individuals who can affect your ability to reach your goals? There is a certain comfort in knowing that when you go to McDonald's, you know what you are going to get. So let the people around you feel just as comfortable by letting them know you for your own personal brand of excellence, your own personal brand of consistency.

#15 ~ Your Thirty-Second Radio Ad

What are your personal strengths? Can you answer this question clearly? Can you answer this question with conviction? Can you answer this question concisely? Can you answer this question in a way that conveys your strengths through unique and powerful words? If you can, then you have already written the thirty-second radio ad to sell who you are to others.

Superman had his personal ad down. He was "faster than a speeding bullet, more powerful than a locomotive, and able to leap tall buildings in a single bound."

Those words paint a clear picture of the superhero. The lesson I am putting forward here is that you cannot sell yourself by using generalities in your personal ad. If Superman were just fast, how impressive would that be? If he was just powerful how awe inspiring would that be? You cannot sell yourself using clichés, as those around you will only say, "I've heard it all before." You only get one chance to make that first impression.

Maybe the time to sell yourself to someone will be today or maybe tomorrow. Question is, *Are you ready? Will your thirty-second ad make a first impression as powerful as that locomotive?*

#16 ~ Advertising Works

It is said that 50 percent of all advertising is effective. This claim then begs us to ask the question, *Which half?* Because, if half of all advertising efforts to persuade are effective, then we can equally assume that we successfully communicate what we say to others only half of the time. What 50 percent is working, and what 50 percent is not?

When we work hard to communicate our ideas effectively, we give ourselves the best chance to become successful in life. Your ideas have no value until you communicate them to someone else. Successful individuals work to develop their ability to communicate with those around them. They are well aware that only one out of two of their words may actually communicate the essence of their thoughts. With this challenge in mind, they double their efforts to ensure they have chosen their words carefully in order to ensure understanding of their ideas.

Confusion that undermines understanding is like an infection out of control. Confusion produced by our inability to communicate effectively can lead all of us to question the very value of an individual and their ideas.

You must know that when your ideas are powered by your focused efforts to clearly communicate them, only then do those ideas have the potential to be seen by others as great ones.

#17 ~ Be the Chameleon

People, you think you know them, then things change, they change. Successful individuals are not only able to adapt to the changing personalities of the people they deal with, but they also use these differences to their advantage.

As a chameleon changes color in response to its environment, your ability to harmonize and reflect the personality types of people you are working with will directly influence your success within that relationship.

You must be able to function with all the dynamically fractured personalities you work with in order to have a positive influence on your own ability to achieve your personal objectives.

When you can read and reflect those differences, you will find your success is in your ability to become the chameleon.

#18 ~ You'll Want to Catch It

Confidence is contagious on many levels. It is all about formulating a *can do* attitude in order to get things done on your own or within the group.

When geese migrate each season, both north and south, they fly in formation behind the leader. To be the goose at the front of your team's formation, you will need to lead through sharing your personal confidence. You can do this by clearly conveying to those around you that you have the ability to take the group where they want to go. Make them believe that together you have all that is necessary to achieve your shared objective.

Beyond that group dynamic, confidence not only spreads from person to person, but it spreads and grows within us as individuals. The real power is in the knowing that you have confidence and believe in your own ability to take yourself to where you want to go.

However, this is also true about how doubt can overcome you or your group. It is important for you to know that both things are true. This knowledge puts you in control of the direction of the flock, which influences your direction as the lead bird in your own migration.

So spread your wealth of confidence with others and allow yourself permission to believe in yourself and all that is possible.

#19 ~ Step Up

No one could or should possibly believe that a single step forward followed two steps back could be considered progress, right?

Wrong! Real progress may require us occasionally to first take those couple steps back. Only then are we able to take our next steps forward. One's ability to gain proper perspective can be a key in their ability to obtain their goals. Sometimes in order to actually gain a true perspective, you must step back from where you are standing. Only then will you be able to see clearly the entire picture.

That is why you should consider adopting the belief that it is not really a step backward if your actions allow you eventually to go forward with confidence.

The challenge for all of us is not so much knowing which direction we are going, but why it is that we are going that direction in the first place!

#20 ~ Can't Say Can't

Your mom and I banned one word from our home while you were growing up. That word was *can't*. Looking back, maybe we should also have wiped a few other words from the family vocabulary. But what the *hell* can we do about that now?

No word in the English language has more power to influence behavior than the word *can't*.

For the most part, I can say that your mom and I were successful in teaching you about the potential sapping power within, what I believe, is the most offensive of all the four-letter words. I have never understood why. The word *can't* is not even considered one of the four-letter words that are traditionally frowned on by our society.

Yet none of those other four-letter words have the potential to create greater personal scarring than the mental scars you suffer when you tell yourself that you do not have what it takes to succeed.

No matter if you are telling yourself that you cannot overcome a roadblock that you believe limits your potential, or if the word *can't* is used by others to define for you what they believe is possible. The word exists as an anchor that leads you to believe that you should not bother to even try.

Maybe you will succeed in reaching all your goals, and maybe you will not. It just should never be because you denied yourself or let others deny you the opportunity to try.

#21 ~ Passion

Your bosses can give you direction. They can help you develop your skills, and they can help you build your knowledge. Nevertheless, at best, all the above support will only result in mediocrity if you do not have real passion for what you do.

Passion is the energy that drives ordinary people to achieve great things. Without driving passion, a talented person will settle for rising to the level of underachiever.

None of my words can give you what you must find for yourself. The good news is that you do not need to look far; you will find that the things that drive you are on the inside. Look inward to find the most powerful emotions to drive your outward behavior.

In the end, the process of unleashing your passion and finding your success is up to you. Your passions are there. You just need to find them and set them free.

Know yourself, and you will certainly know what emotions have that power to take you anywhere you want to go.

#22 ~ Birds of a Feather

I thought that everyone understood and believed that *opposites attract*. Yet, people seem to feel perfectly comfortable with the old saying, "Birds of a feather flock together."

So I ask you, do you think that things that are alike attract each other, or do you think it is true that opposites attract? I think the answer is that it depends. I know one thing about this contradiction for sure, that is, successful people not only can deal with these opposing points of view, but they have the power of perception necessary to take advantage of the difference.

In a situation where birds are flocking, successful individuals may be looking to find their strength in the support of those around them as they look to leverage the power of their shared ideological convictions.

When opposites are attracting, successful people are looking to find even greater strength in their ability to offset their personal weaknesses with other people's strengths.

Just as a good speaker knows their audience, people looking to reach specific goals should also understand the perspective of those around them. No matter whether those people are different or the same, you will find success in any relationship as long as you understand where it is that person is coming from and where it is they want to go!

#23 ~ It's Not Fair

Do you want to be right? Just say to yourself, *It's not fair!* and you will be right about most things most of the time.

Do you want to be happy? Just accept that it is not fair!

I hope that everyone is raised with some general sense of what is right, wrong, or fair in any given situation. You could call that general sensibility, your moral compass.

Success is a product of our ability to set our moral compass and then follow it along life's path without getting lost along the way.

For many of us, the biggest roadblock to our own happiness is our need to take responsibility for making things around us right; fixing what is not fair. Our compass sets our values and leads us to want to get involved in order to make it right. (I would consider that this need for me to get involved in trying to fix things is my greatest personal weakness, or I could say it is my greatest personal strength.)

Compassion is a gift, and it can be a curse. Take my advice here and know that you cannot fix all that is wrong with the world. Endeavor to act fairly, try to do what is right, and accept the fact that not everyone in every situation will strive, as you should, to claim the moral high ground.

#24 ~ I Need a Ride

When you were nine years old, *being driven* meant only that one of your parents was taking you to a friend's house in the car. Now you are the one responsible to provide yourself proper transportation toward the success you seek.

Although you can, from time to time, still hitch a ride with a friend, it is now your main responsibility to secure and maintain the level of personal drive necessary to succeed.

It is easy to say, "I want to become a _____." It is up to you to fill in the blank. Yet only you are in a position to make that happen. When you were young, your parents tried to provide you the impetus, say motivation, to encourage you to be a successful trumpet player, great volleyball player, or straight-A student. Oops, I guess you cannot win them all!

However, as you grew older, you could almost feel as the responsibility for your own success was passed off to you by your mom and I. Today your success is all in your hands. The question is, *Do you have the drive to get yourself there?*

#25 ~ Keep It in Your Ledger

The perfect tool to help you build your positive self-image is a *success ledger.* In general, a ledger is an accounting tool where you record your deposits and withdrawals, your assets and liabilities. However, a success ledger is a place where you only record your personal wins, your own strides forward, your successes.

Your success ledger is a record upon which you can look back, in order to justify and support your high level of self-esteem. It is this kind of record keeping that will allow you to maintain your *always forward* self-confident attitude.

You build your self-confidence over time through the process of internalizing each of your personal successes. You can aid this process through the commitment to maintain your own record of personal accomplishment. By having a place in which you document your own success, you automatically heighten your awareness of all the things that you have successfully accomplished.

It is each of your accomplishments, when recognized by your own self, which will help you to define yourself as the successful individual you strive to be.

#26 ~ Call Your Mom

There never seems to be a shortage of people willing to offer you advice, even when you are not interested in getting any. Can you say the word *parents?* Now I know you understand how important it is to be open to new ways of thinking. However, from time to time, you can actually be successful at navigating life's maze of challenges all by yourself. By yourself I mean, without much extra help.

An all-pro quarterback receives more advice than anyone could possibly assimilate on the Monday morning sports talk shows. Is it all well-meaning? No, it is not. Are those fans right? Well, sometimes.

To be successful, you need to be able to deal with the unsolicited direction you are sure to receive. You need to be able to sort through the chaff of bad advice to get to the wheat of the good. On the flip side of the coin you also need to know when to keep your own advice to yourself.

If you are going to give it, you had better be able to take it. You will only find your real success when you have the confidence to consider different points of view and are not afraid to change your mind, take the good advice, and leave the rest behind.

However, certain advice is always good advice . . . call your mom!

#27 ~ Consistency Counts

Perhaps you think that flowers thrive with a consistent diet of sunshine and warmth. In reality it is the inconsistency of the April showers that make those pretty May flowers possible.

When you are looking toward your goals, you should remember that, typically, flowers could not grow with either consistent sun or consistent rain. However, as you strive to reach the success you desire, you need to remember you are not a flower and that the people around you are not flowers. People, unlike the flowers, find comfort in life's consistency.

What I am getting at is that in order for others to see you as successful, you should first look to have them view you as consistent. The people around you will flourish when there is some degree of predictability to what your reaction to specific situations will be. It is not that your reaction to the unforeseen challenges around you should be less than creative. It is that your responses to the day-in and day-out situations need to be perceived as consistent. Some use the terms *level-headed* or *even-keeled.*

Within this environment of consistency, you will quickly learn that the people around you will see that you are a person they can trust. With the trust of those around you, together all of you will certainly be more successful.

#28 ~ Live, Laugh, Love

It is up to you to strive for all the things that are important to you if you wish to achieve them.

With that in mind, let me remind you that it is up to you to find the balance that makes you happy within your own life. Find a balance that allows you to make time for work, for friends, for family, and for God! (Not necessarily in that order.)

Unless you awake every day with this responsibility on your mind, you risk becoming out of balance, and missing those little things in life that lift the spirit and lighten the heart.

You have to know that you only go through life once, and you do not want to risk ever feeling the need to look back wishing for something different from what you have found.

So get out there and live, laugh, and love every day.

#29 ~ Let's Compromise

Give and take, that is the process by which civilized adults with differing ideas and differing ideals work together in order to achieve mutual goals. As you might guess, I am not talking about the United States Senate here.

What you need to understand is that there is a difference between the idea of compromising your position to achieve your goal and compromising your values to do the same. To protect your values and your integrity, you must clearly understand for yourself where to draw the line that you will not cross.

That is not being stubborn; rather, it is just being principled. When you compromise your values, you end up compromising who you really are.

Understand that in your search for the middle ground of compromise, you should never give up your higher moral ground. Just draw your line in the sand and then be willing to stand your ground, and you will be seen as a person of integrity.

#30 ~ Divide and be Conquered

You cannot be married to one person and date another without diminishing your commitment to the person to whom you are married.

You cannot be successful in life when your commitment to excellence is distracted by conflicting thoughts, misdirected ambitions, and unclear goals.

Conflicting thoughts can lead you to doubt who you are and what you want from life. Misdirected ambitions have you chasing those things that will not help you get what you are really looking for. Unclear goals leave you lost without a vision of how you will define your success.

By definition, when your commitment to excellence is divided, you can no longer be said to be committed. Without your total uncompromising commitment, your quest to conquer your goals will most likely fail.

#31 ~ I Want, I Want, I Want

Until you take a child to the grocery store, you have no idea how annoying the mantra of "I want, I want, I want" can be. Until you take a young child to the toy store, until you go anywhere with a young child, you may miss this very important lesson regarding how to, in the end, be happy in life.

You can only be happy when you allow yourself to be happy with who you are and what it is you have. Now many people confuse an individual's drive to be successful with their own focused effort to satisfy a personal *I want*.

Of course, all your goals could be translated into one form or another of I want. Yet, I am not suggesting you gear back that level of personal drive to achieve what is important to you. One thing you should realize is that the most toys, the biggest house, or the most extravagant vacation should and never will define your success.

The reality is that you risk your long-term happiness by tying it to your ability to check off each of the items on your personal I want list. You risk never being at peace, never being satisfied, never being happy inside or out.

You cannot be successful if you are not happy, and I want you to be happy. (This *I want* does not count because I want this for you.)

#32 ~ Don't Have Favorites

Life is too short to have favorites. Yes, you heard me! Odd, I know, but stop for a moment, and you will realize that the concept of favorites is nothing more than a trap that limits your life's experience. The concept of favorites as *the best,* in the end will diminish your willingness to choose differently and experience all that is new.

Even having favorites should call in to question your ability to make such a claim in the first place. How can you credibly celebrate something as a *favorite* when chosen from a short list of limited experiences?

When you always order your favorite food at a restaurant, you will never experience the very something on the menu that might just be a bit more amazing.

To always vacation at your favorite place makes it certain you will never discover the rest of the world you have never before seen.

To always rewatch your favorite movies, listen to your favorite song, and reread your favorite book is guarantee that in the end you will become bored with the repetition.

Find your joy in the discovery of what is new, different, and hopefully better. See your definition of success as having lived life so fully that you have an endless list of favorites.

#33 ~ Four~Letter Word

Some would say that, "All things in life are selling." You might have heard me say that . . . ohhh, say once or twice.

At the same time, it is only possible for *sell* to be something more than a four-letter word when it is something you do with other people, not something you do to them.

Of course, we want our own way. I guess that is human nature. However, when we work to sell others on ideas that only benefit our own interests, we can clearly see how sell is seen as a dirty little four-letter word.

Is a feeling of real success possible when our success does not bring benefit to the individuals who help us to get there? When you find yourself needing to oversell an idea, you should then realize that what you probably are promoting is something that truly will only benefit yourself.

Your mom always taught you that intelligent people do not need to use four-letter words. I could add that truly successful people do not use them either.

#34 ~ Judge for Yourself

Others scrutinize everything we do each day. Our intentions are measured, our efforts are measured, and our results are measured. That makes everyone wonder how he or she personally measures up.

It is a lot of power we give to others when we let them pass judgment on us, or should I say when we accept the judgments they pass.

We all do it . . . judge, that is. What a great cause! What a great effort! What a great performance! Yes, we all do it. We judge others, and we judge ourselves. That's ugly! That's terrible! That's rude!

Success does begin with our good intentions. It grows from our extra effort, and we earn it through our achievement of extraordinary results!

However, in the end, you will have to judge it all for yourself! So let me ask, *Do you measure up?*

#35 ~ Eat Like a Chicken

My grandfather Murly DeByle once told me, "You can't shit like an eagle when you eat like a chicken." (Sorry, his words.)

After many years of contemplation of those words, I now see the analogy as telling me that you cannot do big things when your actions limit your potential.

It has to make you wonder as to how your actions may be limiting your potential. Maybe this is what they mean when they say that in order to be successful, sometimes people only need to get out of their own way. In some cases, only by removing the limits people set for or on themselves are they able to reach the success they desire.

Think big! Poop big! Both really represent the same thing. You have to do more than talk the talk. For big things to happen, you need to be willing to walk the walk. As Nike says, "Just do it."

Now that you understand, stop going through life trying to peck your way to the top, as everyone knows the chicken will never be king of the hill. Do not be the chicken. Be the eagle, and you will soar to the top!

#36 ~ I Dare You

The three-word challenge, *I dare you*, is what one little kid says to a friend when they want them to jump off the roof, sneak out of the house, or play spin the bottle.

The words *I dare you* are the modern-day equivalent of throwing down the gauntlet in medieval times. When you take the dare, you give away control of the situation. I say it is okay to take a dare. However, only do so when you are given the chance to decide if that decision is one you are making for yourself.

When you are the one to challenge your own status quo, you are the one who clarifies your own personal definition of success. You do this through the achievement of the goals you have set for yourself. You are the one who has the power to control your own course. But only when you refuse to give up your own dreams in deference to the dreams others dare you to dream.

Pick up the gauntlet laid down by others only when it matches your vision for what you want to accomplish and only when it helps define the person you want to be. Otherwise, issue your own challenge to yourself, then go out and meet those challenges as those achievements will define your success!

#37 ~ Weakest Link

As people, we resemble a chain, each of us made up of individual links that represent each of our individual strengths and weaknesses.

We rely on our strengths to carry the load, and we work to ensure that our weaknesses will not be the cause of our failure.

Yet, we are all well aware of the saying, "A chain is only as strong as its weakest link." By taking the time and closely examining the links within your own chain, you will come to clearly know and understand your strengths and weaknesses. It is with this understanding that you empower yourself to go forward and build a chain of ever-increasing strength.

Take a closer look at the links of the chain that define who you are. Then strive to change the necessary links in order to become the person we want to be. Without your focused effort to grow as an individual, one link at a time, your chain will remain unchanged.

Today is the day to make the critical commitment to forge the new links in the chain that will represent a better, stronger you.

#38 ~ Juggler or Clown

Even the professional jugglers routinely drop one of the objects they endeavor to keep in the air. You might say they had taken on more than they could handle.

Therefore, if it is your objective to juggle all the responsibilities in your life, you must decide what you can successfully juggle without appearing to be the clown. Knowing your limitations is as important as the effort you put forth in stretching your abilities. We draw the line between success and failure at one's ability to know when to step forward and when to step back.

Know that it is okay to add a ball to the responsibilities you juggle when you feel the need to stretch your potential. Nevertheless, you need to be prepared to set responsibilities aside when it becomes evident that achieving excellence is temporarily out of your reach.

#39 ~ Sacrificial Lamb

When we prepare the sacrificial lamb for its sacrifice, you can be sure that the lamb knows that it will be the only one who will sacrifice anything that day.

It can be like that in relationships. That is, sometimes, one person in the relationship is the person who is called on to always sacrifice their dreams, their desires, and their hopes in deference to the other.

It is clear to me that in a real sacrificial ceremony, I would rather not be the lamb. Just as in life, you should never be satisfied with being the one who always gives in. You need to ask yourself why you are the one who always sacrifices that which is important to them.

Each of us must sacrifice from time to time for the benefit of our friends, family, and coworkers. Ask yourself just how often are you the one who is asked to lie upon the cold executioner's stone. The answer to this question may affect your willingness to be the sacrificial lamb the next time others call on you to sacrifice your own dreams and desires.

Look for and provide equality and balance within your relationships; only then will your giving in not be seen as a sacrifice.

#40 ~ It's a Secret

The choice is yours. In order for you to reach your personal goals in life, either you can choose to work harder, or you can choose to work smarter.

Well, at least that is the commonly held belief. Let me share with you the secret held by many successful people. It is simple. Successful people know that working smart sometimes requires that they work hard. Hardly seems fair, does it? You see, their secret is that they know when they sometimes will need to do both, work hard and work smart in order to be successful.

It should now be clear to you. These two choices are not mutually exclusive. That is why you need to prepare yourself for those opportunities in life when it becomes necessary to work both harder and work smarter in order to take a giant step toward your goals, your success, and your happiness!

#41 ~ Find the Coat Hook

Self-confidence is the fuel that drives everyone's ability to define themselves as successful. Without the empowerment created by this emotional engine, your ambitions will be out of gas!

As a parent, I saw that my main responsibility was to find a coat hook upon which each of my kids could hang their self-confidence. In order to accomplish this job, I needed to help them each find something that they were good at doing. That is, to help them develop a talent or skill that could be the basis of the self-confidence they would need in order to move forward in years to come.

Now you are out on your own, and you need to be aware of the importance of the coat hooks I have helped you find and the ones you have developed all on your own. You need to understand not only how important a role your self-confidence has played in your success so far, you also need to understand how fragile it can be.

With that being so, as you go forward, you must always be mindful to keep your coat hooks filled, so as to support the personal confidence necessary in your efforts each day to succeed.

#42 ~ Whatever it Takes

What are you willing to do in order to become as successful as you want to be?

You have to know that whatever road you have chosen to travel in life, finding success will require an incredible level of personal commitment. As only through your commitment to that journey will you be able to successfully travel the length of your chosen road.

I want to tell you without any reservation that I have found only one philosophy that will guarantee the achievement of all your goals. You must be willing to do *whatever it takes*!

Occasionally, there are those who may find success at the end of a very short road. Nevertheless, I urge you not waste your time looking for the shortcut to happiness. Just be willing to do whatever it takes to get those things that you want out of life, and the road will always call you lucky.

#43 ~ The Reward for Loyalty

Loyalty has its rewards, not just the type of reward where you get the eleventh sandwich free because you paid for the ten before it. The loyalty that I am talking about is the kind of reward you find in the security of friends and coworkers. Those are the individuals whose loyalty you earn as reward for always having their backs.

Loyalty is not a given, it is a reward that you earn over time, and it is essential in order for you to build relationships worth having.

A dog is loyal—unquestioningly so. I am not suggesting you need to be anyone's lapdog. But your loyalty will be rewarded and your relationships enhanced by the respect your returned personal loyalty represents.

For a dog, you reward their type of loyalty with a belly scratch, a biscuit treat, or a morning walk. If you want to find your own reward, be as loyal as man's best friend. Rewarded not by playing a game of Fetch the Stick but by the feeling of success that comes from having the kind of friends you can count on.

#44 ~ ASS of U and ME

We have all heard the old saying, "When you assume something, it's likely that you will make an *ass of you and me*." Maybe we think that we have heard it so many times that we have learned its lesson.

Yet day after day, we find ourselves in a position to think that we know what is right, to think that we know what will happen next, and to think that our specific actions will result in certain results.

Each day, we assume we know the right thing to do in order to be successful. The problem is, the game of life is always changing. We mistakenly find ourselves thinking we know what to do. Yet in the end, we often end up making an ASS of U and ME.

We are certain that what has worked in the past will work again. That is why we jump blindly to the conclusion that the situations are the same. Confidence is a very powerful emotion. Yet it can backfire when that confidence leads you to assume you know more than you might.

Do not be afraid to ask the same questions a second time. You will be surprised to find that, occasionally, the answer will not end up being what you thought.

#45 ~ Ya Gotta Have a Penny

The pyramids were built one stone at a time.

The race is run one stride at a time.

Your personal wealth will be amassed one penny at a time.

I believe that "you've got to have a penny before you can have a dollar." This is the clearest advice on building financial and personal success ever declared, and I am proud to say that I'm certain that I made it up.

The *penny first* rule, as I'll call it, is the lesson found in our need to recognize that we can create nothing large without first taking smaller incremental steps. Those who built the pyramids needed to move the first stone into place before they could place the capstone.

In becoming successful in the realm of personal finance, you must first earn that first penny, nickel, dime, and quarter before you can focus on your first dollar, twenty, hundred, thousand, or million dollars.

In your search for all the levels of financial success you desire, you can easily lose focus of the basics. That is, if you want to have a dollar, you must first save a penny.

Just know that you can eventually achieve all great things in life through a similar degree of incremental success.

#46 ~ I See the Real You

Your image is everything! That statement is true only if it reflects who you really are. Like the veneer on the dining room table, a false image is thin and less durable than the thick solid oak of who you really are.

With that thought in mind, my advice to you is, do not build your image on the shaky ground of self-promotion. Rather, build your image on your history of accomplishment and reputation for follow through.

Solid wood veneer is able to be milled so thin that you are actually able to read these words through it. Yes, veneer is actually solid wood. Yet similar to the image people falsely create for themselves, it is possible that you too will find it easy to see through.

Do not project a false image of yourself in hopes that it will be well received. Project yourself as you really are. You may be surprised when others find the richness of the grain of the real you to be so much more beautiful than the person you tried to be.

#47 ~ Success Junkie

Are you looking for a quick fix for your life's challenges? Then you are a *success junkie*.

Great success does not come without hard work, sacrifice, commitment, and focus. Yet these are not words familiar to the success junkie. Junkies talk in terms of luck, hope, wishes, and tomorrow. They look backward rather than forward, and their favorite two words are *if only*.

Looking for an easy way to make it through life is the journey of the junkie. You see, the junkie is just looking to get by, to make it to the weekend, and to make their next big score.

You will never see a junkie planning for their future because they do not believe that the future is in their control.

Therefore, leave the junkies behind and go the extra mile necessary to find your success!

#48 ~ Justify Then Decide

Life's decisions do not always derive from what you could call a logical order of thought. To see this more clearly, follow along with this somewhat typical human decision-making process.

Your friend has a big-screen tv. This makes you think how nice it would be to have one too. You decide that you want a big-screen tv. You decide that you would be happier if you owned a big-screen tv. You tell yourself that you would be happier because your family would enjoy more time together. You decide that by spending more time as a family, your kids would be less likely to get into trouble. Then with all that decided, you go to your significant other and say, "I'm worried about the kids. I think they're at risk of getting in trouble since we don't spend enough family time, and we could fix that if we got a big-screen tv!"

In the process of making a decision, we often decide first and then we justify, justify, justify. We justify to the point where we begin to convince ourselves that we arrived at our thoughtful decision based purely on our flawless rationale.

You will not find success in a decision-making process based on justified logic driven solely by emotion. That is because you only find success through your own thoughtful consideration of all the pluses and the minuses within your decisions. To make your decisions in any other manner is simply justification.

#49 ~ Chicken or the Egg

The question people ask again and again with no definitive answer is, *Which came first, the chicken or the egg?*

Yet the answer to the question of what comes first in the creation of successful relationships is easy. In order to be liked, to be loved, to be trusted, and to be respected, you must first endeavor to sell yourself to others.

Is it the chicken or the egg, you ask? In the realm of relationships, it is all about you. You come first by default as no one was in the market to buy you today. Thus, your job then is to try to sell them on why you, why they should care.

In relationship building, individuals subconsciously ask themselves the question of why they should invest themselves in you. I ask you to consider what your value proposition as a person is. Ask yourself, Am I a good listener? Determine if your experience can help others be more successful. Decide for yourself if you will be there when they need you.

I submit that your value proposition is you, all of who you are. Now that raises the question of how you can clearly define who you are as a person. Many people attempt to define themselves through mere words. Just know that the answer to this question of why you, is most clearly offered in the honesty of your everyday actions.

#50 ~ Don't Stand on Stupidity

What you know or, should I say, what you think you know is always open to question. I suggest that in order to reach the success you desire, you never *stand on stupidity!*

To stand on stupidity is my own way of suggesting that failure will most certainly be found when you fail to open your mind. You need to consider the possibility that in any given situation, others just might be right and that you might be wrong.

People who stand on their stupidity are those who find themselves firmly planted—contrary to all reason—in opposition to what clearly are better answers. The stupidity comes in when a person continues to argue a point where, if given sincere consideration, they would end up having to admit later that they were wrong.

Do not let personal pride get in the way of your personal success. Changing your mind is nothing more than an admission that you have the intelligence and desire to learn from those around you.

#51 ~ Power of Commitment

No level of success can fail to be achieved through the efforts of an individual committed to a goal. For those individuals, no obstacle can stand in the face of their commitment to overcome all that comes their way.

You will find that commitment is the first step on your journey to success. So begin your journey by making a commitment to yourself to surpass your goals and exceed the expectations of others.

Never look back, hesitate, or waiver. Make a commitment today to live life to the fullest, and success will find you wherever you choose to travel.

#52 ~ Buyer Beware

Fool me once, shame on you . . . Fool me twice, shame on me.

Cynicism surrounds us all. Even my writing that statement here is proof in part of the fact. What this means is that when you talk, the people around you are distracted by their doubt. Their fear of being fooled makes them inclined to question your motives. They may wonder, *What does she really want?*

You probably will never be able to change the outlook of the entire world around you. However, you can strive to justify the trust others may choose to bestow on you one person at a time.

It is like the old saying goes, "You're either part of the problem, or you're part of the solution." When it comes to the world's *integrity gap,* you need to strive to be part of the solution.

You can bridge that gap of trust by showing the people with whom you surround yourself that they can dare to actually trust again. You need to show them that there are still people worthy of believing in, and you are one of them!

#53 ~ Make it Count

What truly successful people do with their lives by definition then makes a difference in the lives of those around them. You must understand that life is about more than just doing. It is about doing for others first then working to be known for what you do. I am not saying that your greatest concern should be the credit you gain from your actions. However, you have an opportunity to define your personal point of difference through your personal compassion for others.

When the thing that differentiates you from those around you is your purpose in life, and your purpose is to make a difference in other people's lives, then you define yourself by how you go about making each day count. When you reach out and touch a life, you really touch two—theirs and your own.

This is what they mean when they say, "You get more than you give."

It is what they mean when they say, "It is more blessed to give than to receive."

When you separate yourself through your acts of kindness and generosity, you will find joy in each and every day.

#54 ~ May the Force be with You

"Different, how will you be?" asked Master Yoda. This *Star Wars* icon kept us all a bit off balance by his ability to turn his sentences inside out. You will more clearly understand Master Yoda's quotation above when you ask it in our more standardized English format, "How will you be different?"

That question is what my dad asked me the day I first told him that I would be leaving our family business. "Different, why do I need to be different?" I asked in reply. His answer changed my life and may have the power to change yours. "Well, if you don't know," he said, "perhaps you're not ready to go."

Those words took me totally off guard. I had just made what was the most difficult decision of my life, and he wanted to know how I would be different. What he was trying to let me know is that I would never find my success within the status quo. It is in how you differentiate yourself that allows you to define your advantage over those with whom you compete.

So answer Master Yoda's question for yourself in order to find your success, "Different, how will you be?"

#55 ~ Sharpen the Axe

You may have read that Abraham Lincoln is credited with the remark, "If I had eight hours to cut down a tree, I'd spend six hours sharpening my axe." In these words, he tells us that proper preparation helps to ensure successful results.

Few of those people with whom you will compete throughout your lifetime will take the necessary time to sharpen their intellect, their product knowledge, or their understanding of their clients' business. Many of those people, with whom you will compete, will not even take time to sharpen their own understanding of their product, company, industry, or themselves.

Based on this, to stay on top, take the time to sharpen your axe. People who prepare to achieve success achieve success more often. This is what I believe the poet Emerson was talking about when he described the road less traveled.

#56 ~ Pit Bull on the Pant Leg

"Let go! Let go!"

Grrrrrrrrrrrrrrrr!

"Let go!" I said.

The pit bull is a symbol of tenacity, and tenacity is one of those traits we find that is the key to grrrrreatness!

Does acceptance of responsibility bring out the pit bull in you? You already know that single-minded focus is a powerful tool in your quest for success. Maybe the above image of the pit bull on the pant leg of a person who is trying to shake it loose will give you a clearer vision of the level of focus you will need in order to succeed.

So get yourself focused and connect with your inner pit bull in order to win in the big game of life.

#57 ~ Words Matter

When I say red, you hear blue. When I say blue, you hear green. Many people mistakenly believe that people all universally understand the words they use. The reality is that words in and of themselves only have some generally accepted sort of meaning as defined for us by *Webster's Unabridged Dictionary*.

In reality, our many cultural differences are what color these symbols of thought with our own personal meanings. Do not get me wrong; the definition in the dictionary is clear and very concise. What is not so clear is our interpretation of the meaning of those words, and that is what creates the confusion. Even with our world's growing cultural commonality, we find that the meanings of our words are often personally shaped more by our own life experiences than anything else.

If a person grew up on a farm in the Midwest, raised by a single parent, was poor, had six brothers, and loved to tend a garden, they would have had a different set of life experiences than you had. Thus, you would have a somewhat different perspective on life.

Let's face it. Our life experiences do affect how we interpret what we mean by the words we use. Yet, however, confidently we may believe that we have actually communicated. The reality is that words, colored by our experiences, will have a degree of a different meaning to each of those around us.

Those who understand this challenge to everyone's ability to communicate will engage in the hard work necessary to achieve true communication and ensure their own individual success.

#58 ~ Right and Wrong

When you are faced with a decision, the result of which will be right for you but so very wrong to those around you, what then ultimately defines the decision as right or wrong? I ask you, how can something that is wrong for so many, in reality, be right at all? Ethically, is it right to climb the mountain that defines our success over the backs of others? Of course, in all games, there are winners and losers. So then, if life is to be thought of as a game, the answer would obviously be yes. We would do what was necessary to win, at all costs.

I'm always amazed that on the reality tv show *Survivor*, players take the efforts of their competitors to win so personally. The premise of the show is to outplay, outwit, and outlast your opponents. That to me says you have permission to do whatever it takes in order to win. The rules of the game are that there are no rules. In my mind, the players who get to the end should be admired for how they played the game. They should be admired for how they misled, cheated, and lied outright to others in order to reach the end. Nevertheless, even in this game based on deception, people still fail to see that doing what is necessary to win is the right thing to do.

Because life really is not a game. I think that true success should be something for which you can be proud. That means your goal would be to create for yourself the kind of success that, like the ocean tide, raises all boats. To consider your success a victory, it does not have to come at the expense of those who are around you. Yes, in a game, there are winners and losers. But in life, you have to ask, isn't it really okay to have winners and winners? Now that is my definition of true success.

#59 ~ Pin the Tail on the Donkey

Without clarity of goals, you will not experience the satisfaction of knowing when you have found success.

Life is not a game of chance where your ultimate achievements are left to accident or luck. As the world spins out of control around us, life's big winners never hesitate. When it is their turn, they step forward boldly, confidently, and stick the donkey squarely in the ass with their tail!

Take the blindfold off and clearly see your goals. Only then can you clearly see to chart the course for your future.

#60 ~ Moving Mountains

The refreshing splash of a spring rain carries with it the power to wash away the greatest mountains on earth one grain of sand at a time.

So too, with similar perseverance, do you have the power to overcome the most imposing of the obstacles in your life. No, you will not solve most of your problems without a struggle. However, over an extended time, you will find the resolution you seek.

The drop of rain does not despair in the face of the mountains' seeming power to persevere. It is the rain's drip, drip, drip of commitment and its sole-minded commitment to persevere that carries away the mountain in that trickle of spring rain.

It would seem impossible that a raindrop can move mountains. However, what is impossible is a mountain's ability to resist such consistent force.

Apply the lesson of the rain when looking to move the obstacles that stand in your way. Know that anything is possible when you possess a relentless commitment to succeed!

#61 ~ You are Not Alone

Surprisingly, you may find that you will not be able to achieve all great things on your own. However, you need to remember that, for the most part, we are all dependent on others to help us reach our goals in life. That interdependence with others gives us the ability to make the two halves greater than the whole. Together, two people can accomplish so much more than would have been possible had they not looked to each other for a helping hand. It is this premise that allows one plus one to equal three.

Do not be afraid to look to those around you and work together with others to make those great things happen. The people with whom we surround ourselves help us clearly define our potential to do great things. If you find that you are uncertain regarding the importance of this interdependence as it relates to success, then you only need remember the challenge of winning the three-legged race at the church picnic.

Victory is only possible through the total sum of all that you are, and all the people in your life have played a role in that success. They have made all the things in your future possible. So associate yourself with people who you view as having the potential for bigger and better things, and together, nothing will be able to hold you back.

Just remember, look at those around you. Without them, you would only be a shell of the person they have helped you become.

#62 ~ That Person in the Mirror

Achieving full credit for your success is elusive until you can accept full responsibility for your mistakes.

When you look in the mirror, you come face-to-face with the only person who can take responsibility for what you do or do not achieve. Now you may be able to mislead all those around you, but you can never really fool that person in the mirror.

So stand up and take responsibility when you are less than successful, and people will gladly give you credit for your achievements when you do achieve success.

#63 ~ People

A successful person has the ability to see the people around them as people. They do not look to use them simply as a means to an end or as a pawn that they manipulate for personal gain.

President Kennedy challenged us all, "Ask not what your country can do for you . . ." My challenge to you is, "Ask not what those around you can do for you, but ask what you can do for them." It is in this level of empathy and compassion where you will find your deepest level of personal satisfaction and your clearest definition of personal success.

#64 ~ Sweat the Small Stuff

If you were on the ledge of a burning building, and across a narrow alley was safe haven, you would contemplate the necessity to risk it all by making the leap in order to save your own life. The distance is not too far—ten feet by your estimate—but looks even farther. Yet it is not the first nine feet eleven inches that will make or break it for you. It is that last inch. If you do not make the last inch, the rest will be history.

So sweat that last inch . . . sweat that small stuff!

Without the will to go the distance, the distance you are willing to go will have no meaning. Only by making it that last inch will you survive the fire and prevent the fall. How then, if such a small difference makes such a big difference, can anyone accept the axiom, *don't sweat the small stuff.*

We have all heard it said that the devil is in the details. If that is so, how can we not sweat the small stuff?

When the horse race of life comes down to a photo finish, will you be seen as having won it by a nose?

Only if you sweat the small stuff will you find the big success that for many remains just out of reach. Remember to sweat the small stuff, and I promise the big stuff will take care of itself.

#65 ~ I Said No . . . Maybe

Sometimes we are forced to say *no* and decline an offer. If circumstances dictate us to say no, then it is clearly wise to accept that conclusion.

However, we are oftentimes put in a situation where we simply do not know how to say yes. That is, we do not know why we should say yes, and so we are only left with the option to say no.

In these instances, you can be subject to a conflict of confidence referred to as *rejecter's remorse*. It is the feeling that you may have mistakenly missed an opportunity to get something better for yourself or your family. You cannot be sure, but your having answered no just doesn't feel right.

Rejecter's remorse is a powerful message from your subconscious telling you that it just might be the right time to change your mind, to reconsider no as your answer. Just like buyers, remorse subconsciously challenges our yes answer.

Self-doubt is natural and should not necessarily be a cause for you to react based solely on that emotional tugging. Yet never be afraid of the subconscious suggestion to change your mind. Nothing has to be forever unless you decide it so.

Remember, when you have blocked your opportunity to move forward by having said no, you can cure your rejecter's remorse by summoning the courage to change your mind and to say *yes!*

#66 ~ Forgive

In order to move forward, you must first stop looking backward so as to avoid being caught up in the trap of past events. Sometimes we simply must be able to forgive and forget if we are to go forward.

By your act of forgiveness, you receive the freedom to put the past behind you. By your forgiveness, you are able to clear away another obstacle in the way of future success, thus freeing yourself to get all that you want from the future to come.

You cannot drive the car down the road looking in the rearview mirror. This means that when your hope is to move forward in life, you must keep your eyes focused forward toward the future.

Anger, bitterness, and/or resentment all anchor you in the past. So I say, "Get over it!" Why, the words themselves even seem to imply that whatever the issue might have been, until you can get over it, it will remain an obstacle. You need to get past the past in order to keep moving forward into the future.

So move on by forgiving those who have wronged you and then forgetting why it all mattered so much in the first place.

#67 ~ Enjoy the Scenery

When we are twelve years old, we cannot wait until we are thirteen, and we become a teenager. Then we again look ahead three years as we anticipate getting our driver's license at age sixteen. Later we are looking forward toward eighteen and next, twenty-one. Great things and wonderful achievements were happening to us along that route, yet much of the time, we failed to find joy in the journey itself.

The mile markers of our life's journey are there to give us an idea of our progress toward where we want to go. These milestones, as it were, provide us a certain level of joy found in our anticipation of their arrival, and we should celebrate those times and their achievement.

Although it is certainly okay to focus on the mile markers, you must never forget to enjoy yourself along the way.

#68 ~ Money Doesn't Equal Success

It is not how much money you choose to make . . . It is how much life you choose to live. Only you have the power to create your own definition of success. So what will it be?

The hardest part about keeping the importance of money in perspective is the fact that we need money to buy many of the things that society has defined as markers for our social success. Those are things such as homes, cars, toys, etc.

Money made in the execution of your job is society's clear definition of your success within your job. Yet that does not reflect the success that we must also achieve in the more personal areas of your life. In those areas, it was clearly understood by the rock 'n' roll band, the Beatles, that "money can't buy you love."

#69 ~ This is Not the End

This is your BEGINNING!

#70 ~ One Last Thought

This is your BEGINNING! Do these words strike you as the promise of what could be, or do you see these words as a warning of the challenges that lie ahead? In either instance, your perception of my meaning for those words would be correct. That is because I meant these words to carry with them a large dose of both hope and reality. No, the sun will not come out every day. The good news, however, is that you won't always find yourself tucked under life's umbrella in order to be shielded against the elements either.

You already know one thing, and that is that the road ahead will certainly be long. All I really can tell you is that the ups and downs that your life's road holds for you, will end in the joy of the great things I'm certain you will achieve one day.

Yes, I know that sounds a lot like it is just your dad talking. However, I really believe that the words on the preceding pages will act as important directions for you to follow on your journey to what will be your hard-earned success.

So what is it that is next for you? Sorry. I cannot tell you that. The ball is now in your court, and although I will always be here for you, I can no longer just kiss it and make it better. When you think about it, isn't that thought amazing? A father can kiss away his daughter's troubles and pain. Then, with nothing more than a gentle touch, he has the power to reassure his little girl and magically make her tears stop.

Kristine, this book might not be able to chase your troubles away like a loving hug. However, I feel confident after the journey I have taken to write it that it has the power to show you the way to make it all better for yourself. The one thing I know for certain, as I write these last words, is that there is as much love in these pages as in any hug or kiss we have ever shared.

My suggestion in the words *this is not the end* carries a more personal meaning to me. That is, these words speak directly to the relationship we have shared all these years. No, your graduation is not the end. No, your moving away will not be the end. No, your finding someone to love forever will not be the end. All these are just a new starting point. It is a point where you still remain my little girl but go forward clearly as a grown woman.

Relationships in general can be complex, but I will always hold dear the simplicity of our relationship with me being your dad and you being my daughter.

Next Level

More Thoughts on the Subject of Success

by Kristine's dad

Dear Kristine,

Today marks the first anniversary of your graduation from college. I believe that you now fully realize that you have had an opportunity to learn more in the last year than was possible over the previous four years. Looking back, it is hard to imagine why college is so expensive, when you leave there still having so much to learn.

Since your graduation, wherever you have gone, whomever you have met, you had a chance to learn something new from the experience. Well, it is the same for all of us. We all have an equal shot at taking away valuable lessons from what life has to teach us. The difference between those who succeed and those who continue to struggle is their commitment to find the lessons. Without that focus and awareness of that opportunity, you will find it hard to take away from those experiences the knowledge needed to achieve your goals.

My first gift to you was a simple collection of my thoughts on the subject of success. I title today's gift, "Next Level: More Thoughts on the Subject of Success." It is simply an additional collection of lessons learned through my life's experience. It is my hope that these additional thoughts will help you to keep the momentum you developed over the last year in the pursuit of your goals. It is my hope that, when put to use, these additional lessons have the potential to take you to the *next level*.

So there you have the evolutionary basis of this book's title. We have all heard it said, "You need to take this to the next level." Personally, I think the conventional idea that you can take your success to another level is somewhat misleading. I believe that when talking on the subject of success, there is truly only one level. Either you are, or you are not successful. Anything less than that just is not, by definition, success.

I see your journey, like everyone's journey to become successful in life, as more marked by milestones. That is, I believe our own personal highway is delineated by what I imagine to be markers alongside life's roadside. Evidence of the validity of my view is the fact that we love to celebrate our personal accomplishments along our chosen road to success. We celebrate all our life's accomplishments, such as graduation, finding true love, working for and getting a promotion, earning respect and receiving acknowledgment. This list could go on for a lifetime, and with some luck and hard work, it will. All these accomplishments are milestones, and we all celebrate each as markers of your success.

Do you see how neat this all fits together? Your goal was to graduate from high school. We celebrated your achievement of that goal as it marked a milestone in your life to that date. Your goal was to earn college scholarships so you could graduate without debt. Your mom and I really celebrated the accomplishment of that goal. Your goal was to land a job in a profession in which you could support yourself and, at the same time, find personal satisfaction. You get a chance to celebrate the accomplishment of that goal every day.

The accomplishment of each and every goal in your life to date has been celebrated as it marked a milestone in your lifelong journey. Then with the momentum of that success pushing you forward, you stood tall upon your accomplishments. With achievement of each successive milestone you were able to boldly look out toward tomorrow and set new and ever-challenging goals. Each accomplishment within your life will mark a milestone on your journey toward your own vision of what success really means to you.

The journey is then, in the bigger sense, made up of the milestones that delineate the accomplishment of your life's short-term goals. A clear example would be the long—and short-term goals of a mountain climber. We understand that their ultimate long-term goal is the top of the mountain. Yet their short-term goals, the milestones of that journey are the next toehold, the next ledge, or the next ridgeline. For the marathoner, the journey is the 26 miles, 385 yards. The milestones are the successive mile markers number one through twenty-six. The shortest-term goals for the runners are each successive stride.

I would like to suggest that when you hear someone challenge you to take it to the next level, that you accept their encouragement; but then do what you need to do in order to meet the personal goals you have set for yourself today. Then with the accomplishment of each new milestone, you further empower yourself to be able to work toward new and greater goals for tomorrow. That is, you can then head out on your journey toward the next marker along life's highway. In the more conventional thought process you can, as they say, take your efforts to what is described as the next level.

If I do not totally buy into the next level idea, then why did I choose this title for the book? It's simple. You already know from what I have written that I believe that success is a journey. I know from our conversations that you also understand and personally believe that to be a fact. That means the base premise upon which we both live our lives is the certainty that achieving personal and professional success is a journey. Let us also agree to our own, slightly different, definition of what the next level means. Not just for the purposes of this book, but our greater purpose is to help us each to get the most out of life. Let us agree that, to you and me, the next level will always represent our personal ability to reach and keep reaching for each of our goals.

Given that thought, I would suggest you look at your journey less in terms of taking your game to the next level. Rather, view it more in terms of focusing on what you need to do next in order to reach the goal you have set for yourself today. To make that happen, you need only to look back to some of the lessons I've shared with you in these books. Yesterday is no longer in the picture. Today you start anew by defining today as the first day of the rest of your life, the next day of your journey. From today forward, you must be in it to win, that is committed to your success, or you will probably always find your short-term goals just out of reach. Unfortunately, this reality would also make your long-term success impossible to achieve.

You might also wonder why these specific thoughts and why now. As you know, we have had many opportunities, since your graduation from college, to discuss the idea of what it takes to succeed. I also know from those conversations that you are well aware that I am still concerned that your managers have left you too much to yourself. That they have failed to live up to their responsibility to help you achieve all the success that is possible. Therefore, those feelings of fear and concern that led to my graduation gift to you a year ago are still on top of my mind and are still weighing heavy on my heart. I can say, however, the difference between then and now is that I am infinitely more confident that you have what it takes to win this game of life. My growing confidence in your eventual success has evolved, despite the fact that I believe you will need to make this journey mostly on your own. As I've often said, your managers have, in my mind, failed to support you with the tools that are necessary. They have abdicated their responsibility to aid in achieving your success. So taking it to that next level is going to have to be up to you.

As the last year has passed, many ideas have crossed my mind. Some are not included here since, in review, they rang a bit too parental in tone. Sorry, it is a bad habit I can't seem to break. However, many of the thoughts here are just as likely as those presented to you in the first book, "Success: My Thoughts on the Subject," to help you reach the individual milestones you seek. In total, they should empower you to reach your own personal next level. In fact, many of the thoughts that follow may be even more powerful than any one of the offerings in that first collection. It is not because they provide greater insight or clearer revelation. It is not because I've become any wiser. I base that statement on my belief in the cumulative ability of all these philosophies to help you to reach your goals. The decision as to whether or not I am right is, in the end, up to you.

My instruction for your use of the materials contained here is still the same as I suggested just a year ago. Take each of these writings for what they are worth. As you know, some will have an immediate impact on you. Some will motivate, some will inspire, while others may fail, at least at this time, to reach out to you and make any impression at all. As I said before, the real secret is to read and reread the words until your maturity or experience allows you to see the power of the thoughts or potentially reveals to you the errors of your dad's way of thinking. I hope it is the first option that you find to be true more often than not.

You have found success on so many levels, and your mom and I could not be prouder. Frankly, I am really looking forward to getting your feedback on the words you find here. I'll be curious to see how your year of experience in the real world may have broadened your perspective and sharpened your insight into what it takes to really be successful. I am curious to hear how or if that experience will make what I have written here any more valuable.

Kristine, I am certain from our ongoing conversations that you no longer see success as a single destination. I believe you see it as the lifelong journey we have so often discussed. That realization is to me the most powerful reason for revisiting the advice which I have to offer you here. Each day, we find ourselves at a different point in our journey through life. Each day, the skills necessary to succeed may be slightly different. As we move forward each day, the perspective from which we view our world changes. Life, for each of us, is ever-changing. So too will be the meaning you find within these lessons.

Is there really a single key to success? Of course, you know that there isn't. Your success will be attained as a culmination of many different aspects of life all coming together. As we said before, it will be a journey. So no, you will not find a magic-bullet answer on how to be successful in this new collection of my thoughts any more than you found a single answer in the last gift I gave you. That is, as you know, because success evolves. Not just from one thing but from different things in every situation. Yes, there are common threads among the ideas I present you. You will find that those connections, represented by the colors of all the yarns woven together, create the beauty of the quilt that will define your success.

So turn the pages here and know that within these pages you will likely find at least one more idea that will be key to your achieving all the things you've ever dreamed of. I promise, you will find at least one thought within the pages that will make rising to your next level of success possible.

Love Always,

Dad

Contents: Next Level

#71 ~ If

Do you find that the word *if* looks forward in hope or back in regret?

"If only they see the value of what I'm saying."
In this case, you can see that the word *if* is looking forward.

"If only I could have worked a bit harder."
Yet here we see that the word *if* is looking back.

It is the same word, but it can lead us in two very different directions. How is it that a simple two-letter word can lead us forward, while at the same time it has the power to hold us back? This one small word has the potential to control our outlook and ultimately affects our ability to find success.

Successful people do not use the word *if* to cling to past failures and perpetuate the resulting regret. Successful people do use the word *if* to anticipate their future achievement.

So take control of your future by using *if* to define all the possibilities that your life has to offer.

#72 ~ This Piece Goes Here

Just as the picture within a puzzle reveals itself by connecting pieces together, your life's story comes together in the same way. The unique pieces of life's puzzle define themselves as the different people, places, and things you experience.

Individuals who you meet for the first time create a basis for their relationship with you by successfully finding a personal connection. You will be most successful when you effectively connect with others by extending yourself, thus giving them an open book sense of who you are. This insight into the real you is not achieved simply by providing others a laundry list of your life's details: born in Wisconsin, raised Lutheran, have one sister, played soccer, was class president.

That connection is to be found within the emotional elements of our life's full and richly detailed experiences. It is through these events that each of us is understood and then seen for who it is that we are. Each of your personal stories has the power to reach out, touch, and connect to those around you. Those experiences, when shared, say more about you than any specific list of your personal statistics or accomplishments.

Since you live your life as an ongoing story of connected successes and failures, you should learn to share yourself through these stories. When you do, your emotionally honest words will act as a personal invitation to others to be a part of your life's yet-to-be-written chapters.

#73 ~ Affirm the Positive

It seems that every book ever written on success touches on the power of personal affirmations.

Repeat after me.

"I am happier and more productive when I plan my day."

"I find I'm more successful when I put the needs and wants of others before my own."

These affirmations can be a subconscious road map to *where* you want to go, *who* you want to be, and *how* you want to get there.

The power of affirmation is in the power of your belief in the words. Tell yourself you are competitive, and you will compete. Tell yourself that you are compassionate, and you will show compassion. Tell yourself that you are the best, and you will strive to be just that.

The power to be the successful person you have hoped to become has been inside of you all the time. So what are you waiting for? Now that you know, just tell yourself what you want most from your life and then go make it happen!

#74 ~ I Can See Clearly Now

No matter what your definition of purpose or clarity of your goals, I see single-minded focus as one of the keys to achieving anyone's definition of what it is to be successful.

If you doubt such wisdom, you should try shooting one arrow at two targets, or you can try laughing and crying at the same time. Try to find equal success smiling while at the same time physically trying to frown.

Life is full of opportunities. Just be sure to take extra care so as not to be distracted and confused by the limitless options in front of you.

Now is the time for you to F-O-C-U-S your energies and to make your best choice.

#75 ~ I Call

In the game of poker, you can end a hand and get the opportunity to see the other person's cards by simply calling their bet. It is the modern day equivalent of a medieval knight throwing down the gauntlet in order to issue a challenge. It is putting your money where your mouth is, proof positive that you believe in yourself. At this point, to beat you, they will have to prove they have the better hand. There, with all the cards on the table, everyone can see who has emerged as the winner.

In life, some people do not want you to call their bet. They want to hold their advantage of the unseen cards. However, in successful relationships like the game of cards, you only know who wins when all the people playing in the game are willing to place all their cards face up on the table.

When you run into a game where one person wants to dominate the table, call their bluff and walk away. I am not talking about poker. I am talking about human relationships and the need for there to be equal give-and-take between partners. Without equality, there is no chance that you will ever be able to call the relationship a success.

Is it fair that one person in a relationship always gets to pick the game? You are good at Texas hold 'em, and they are good at 5 Card Stud. Should you have to settle for always having to play 5 Card Stud?

If you have a winning hand, go all in. However, for a winning relationship, you want two people to be content with never raising their bet.

#76 ~ When the Fat Lady Sings

There is a great difference between a temporary defeat and a total failure. Your ultimate success in life is to be found in your ability to recognize this fact and then to act accordingly.

In sports, the whistle blows, and the game ends. At that particular moment in time, we find ourselves with a clear winner and a clear loser. Yet a losing team or an individual who has lost can snatch success from failure. They can do this through realizing that this loss is nothing more than a temporary defeat.

However, in life, the game does not have a whistle, a bell, or a buzzer to signal, *game over*. The game of life is an ongoing experience where the whistle never blows, and moments of defeat and failure stand seemingly side-by-side.

Once again, you can claim success when you realize that credible options for your victory are still available.

You will see that all things become possible when the lessons you have learned through failure are used as stepping-stones to your second chance for success.

This means that in real life, the fat lady never sings!

#77 ~ Golden Rule

True success in life can be experienced, firsthand, through your helping other people achieve success in whatever they do.

It is very basic. When you take the time and make the effort to help other people get what they want from life, you will get what you want.

What I am saying within this lesson is telling you first to give of yourself to others. It is only when you give first, that you will experience firsthand that the result of giving unselfishly to others is that all good things will come back to you.

The painful reality is that if you choose not to heed this advice, and you thoughtlessly put yourself first, you will often find that you are at the head of a very short line.

#78 ~ All or Nothing

We do not measure integrity by degrees. In other words, you cannot claim to be 90 percent honest. A person is either honest, or they are not; it is all or nothing.

Like virginity, either you are a virgin, or you are not. Once you give up your integrity in the eyes of those around you, you will always be without it.

Now it is certainly clear that all people eventually give up their virginity. It does not have to be equally certain that you will want to or need to give away your integrity to become successful.

Many people struggling to be successful feel that in order to reach their goals, they need to take a bit of creative license with the truth. They may be right in believing that over the short run a little creative embellishment may help them get what they want.

Nevertheless, even though your choice to maintain your integrity may create short-term challenges, your personal reputation as a person with integrity will be a huge advantage to you over time!

Therefore, the rule is, no fooling around, as you will always be too young to lose your integrity!

#79 ~ Better Mousetrap

They say that when you build a better mousetrap, the world will beat a path to your door. Does this mean that your only chance for success in life is to build the better mousetrap? I doubt it, as proven by the many inventors who have conceived and built that better mousetrap, only to fail in their efforts to sell them profitably.

Maybe it is because the proven consistency of the traditional mousetrap has always trumped the unproven claims of superiority by the latest and greatest. Maybe this means that there is more to achieving success than just trying to be smarter and stronger.

I do not bring this up to divert your quest for excellence in traditional terms of good-better-best. However, I am certain that the better mousetrap would meet sales goals if its inventors would or could only position it as being the better value. That is, value as defined by a product's consistent productivity divided by that product's price.

If this is true, for you to establish yourself as successful, you need to be recognized for the consistency of your own personal performance. This would become your own personal value statement as it were.

Of course, what I am saying here is true. The proof is in the fact that for years it has been the concept of consistent value that has been at the very core of the sales pitch used to sell that old mousetrap.

#80 ~ Dress for Success

There are two racks displaying fur coats in two different stores. In the first store, the rack features fur coats in four distinctive styles. The soft lights warmly illuminate the rack in front of you, with each coat displayed on an expensive wooden hanger stained to match the wood of the display rack. You grab for the price tag and are amazed that a coat of such quality could only cost $599.99.

The second store features that same fur coat. The chrome round rack it hangs on is full and tightly merchandised. The fluorescent lighting reflects off the shiny metal of the rack and its plastic hangers. As you check the price, you are amazed that a coat that you thought was certain to be a great value was outrageously priced at almost $600.

It is the same coat, and it's the same price. Clearly though, there is a different and intended difference in the perception of the coat's value. One perception was intentionally influenced to drive sales. While the perception of that coat being overpriced was an unwanted result of the lack of attention to detail by the store selling it.

How do you display your product? That's you! You are the product. You are responsible for selling each and every day. Do others perceive you as an incredible value, or are you seen as overpriced? You can create the perception of added value both by what you say and do. When they say, "dress for success," they are merely saying that you can also enhance the perception of your value by how you visually present yourself.

You already know that you influence others by what you say and do. Yet only your professional appearance has the ability to positively impact others well before you utter a single word or take a single action.

#81 ~ Look for the Open Door

No matter how much you plan, how hard you focus, or what your level of commitment, you will, at one point or another, stumble and fail. Not fail as in your losing a game of Monopoly. However, at some point, you will likely experience *catastrophic failure* in your life. That is failure of the type that will make you wonder how you can ever possibly move forward tomorrow from such a low point.

Okay, now that you are feeling optimistic about your prospects, let me tell you how it is that you will have the courage to get up off the canvas. Even after life throws you its best knockout punch, you can get back up again. To do it, you look for the open door!

Many successful people face down adversity certain in the fact that when one door closes, another door will open. I, too, believe this to be true. I have seen the powers of the open door at work in my life. Yet if this idea is true, then why doesn't everyone successfully prevail over life's challenges? The answer is simple. They fail to look for or recognize the open door.

When you are down, never count yourself out. Just open your eyes and be ready when the next door opens!

#82 ~ Opportunities Abound

Opportunities may abound, but the courage to make the most of them after they have been discovered is rare. Therefore, I say, "Be courageous!"

The idea that *we've always done it this way* does not delineate a path to greater success. It may merely mark the path of least resistance.

I urge you always to look ahead for opportunities to find your own way, to chart your own course. At the same time, you should also realize that just because a path is well worn does not make it a poor choice to travel. That is the coward's choice, if you will.

Just know that it is your conscious awareness of the choices you make along life's journey that clearly mark the path of your first steps toward the rewards you seek.

#83 ~ Making Friends

Making friends is a process that for some is as easy as falling off a chair. Yet for others, making friends is as daunting as a visit to the dentist. That idea personally makes me squirm just thinking about it.

The task of making new friends does not have to pose such a negative, imposing specter. In fact, making friends can be easy when you employ the old 80-20 rule. That is, when you meet someone with whom you hope to become friends, just focus and spend at least 80 percent of your time together talking about them.

People love to talk about themselves, and that is a fact. In addition, we almost have to feel more positive about the people who personally express an interest in who we are and what we have to say.

To make friends, it is a three-step process: ask questions, shut up, and listen!

As time goes on, they will most certainly run out of stuff to say, and you will get your chance to talk. In the meantime, you will have made a positive impression in the mind of that person, and by then, you will probably have made a friend.

So when it is important for you to make a positive impression with the people you meet, just remember 80-20.

#84 ~ Prince Charming

For her dreams to come true, the princess must be willing to kiss the frog in order for her to find Prince Charming.

Who wants to kiss a frog? Oftentimes in life, we are faced with the need to do the thing we least like in order to get the thing we most want.

We all have dreams, and we all have frogs that are there for us to kiss in order for us to continue along our road to success. Not real frogs, mind you, nor the frogs that you often find in fairy tales. We define these frogs as those tasks we dislike so much that many of us are willing to forgo our dreams just because we do not want to kiss that frog.

When we avoid doing those things within our lives, jobs, or relationships that we know we need to do in order to achieve success, we've given into the worst form of self-defeating avoidance and procrastination.

Kiss the frog already! Your *happily ever after* awaits you.

#85 ~ Positive Thinking

A positive attitude makes a difference. Not just in how you see the world, but in how the world sees you. It is a positive attitude that allows you the confidence to always search for the rainbow at the end of the storm.

Positive thinking may be nothing more than your own belief that your efforts will make a difference. Being positive is not synonymous with wishing things to be true. Positive thinking is at the epicenter of the positive energy inside you that allows you to make things happen for yourself.

When you act on that positive energy, you control what happens, rather than being dependent on others to make good things happen for you.

So dare to be positive, while many of those around you are doubtful. Be bold, brazen, and strong in your belief that you can have a positive effect in making it a better tomorrow.

#86 ~ Learning from Our Mistakes

Failure is not just a destination that we reach despite our efforts to create a different, more positive result. Failure is simply a person's inability to see their role in the journey.

By clearly defining your goal as a destination, you can begin to see what you and those around you need to do in order to make it all happen.

In the end, we find that much of failure is simply rooted in our being lost. When you know who you are and what you want, I promise, you will not lose your way on life's journey to find success.

#87 ~ Unleashed Potential

Many of us live within the imaginary boundaries that exist only in our mind, and yet we are afraid to cross them. We, without putting up a struggle, also let others work to build fences that will redefine and limit our real potential.

To unleash your potential, you simply need to understand that the fences representing those mental limitations are not real. To achieve your success, you start by purposefully tearing down the imaginary boundaries that limit your self-perception.

Always stand guard against those who would look to fence you in. Once you accept what you believe to be your limitations, in reality you become bound by those imaginary fence lines you have built for yourself. When that happens, then the success you seek will readily be reachable for only those people who have rejected those same limitations and now find themselves on the opposite side of the fence from you.

#88 ~ Measure Up

What is it that you believe in?

What do you stand for?

The definition of who you are will take more than mere words to define. We personally can be defined by what we say, but we are measured by what we do. Are your words and your actions in sync with the person you want to be? Do you, as they say, *walk the walk?*

We pave the road to failure in life with our good intentions. Intentions otherwise known as the promises we have broken to others. More importantly, the promises broken to ourselves are the base of that failure. Of course, every road will have its bumps and cracks. Yet life's smooth ride is paved by the perception of ourselves in the minds of those around us.

When we act in contradiction with our own selves, we cannot be in connection to that which makes us happy. This persistent incongruity makes certain our inability to achieve those things that we set as our goals.

So put your money where your mouth is by living up to all that you aspire to be.

#89 ~ Word of Advice

Love . . . unconditionally!

Okay, that's two words.

#90 ~ Balancing Act

First, you make your money, and then you spend your money. Make it, spend it, make it, spend it, budgeting becomes a balancing act!

When the juggler tries to keep too many balls in the air, the consequence of that folly is that he is bound to drop one or two as he finds himself out of balance. When you spend more money than you make, the result is that your life becomes out of balance, and the consequence is a *freedom-crushing* debt.

However, I am not saying that the reward earned as the result of success cannot be savored without guilt. Yet, when you claim your rewards before you achieve the results, your result is debt. That kind of debt results from one day finding yourself and your life out of balance due to your wrongful prioritization of your financial assets. The resulting debt is crushing in terms of both costing you focus and crushing in terms of added pressure.

So make it, save it, spend it. Just make sure you find yourself a balance you can live with.

#91 ~ It's All Inside You

The successful ending you strive for must be the ending you see for yourself. You will not find the same motivation to reach a goal unless that goal is truly your own and not just the expectations of those around you.

The motivation necessary to achieve success can only come from inside. Sure, people can encourage you. Sure, people can cheer you on. However, the effort and the drive to succeed only comes from inside.

Yes, leaders lead, and mentors guide. Yet true success, as a result of your efforts, can only be achieved when their goals for you and your goals for yourself are in sync with each other.

Success is a result of focused effort over time. No one can be expected to show the commitment necessary to succeed if they do not fully want someone else's definition of success for themselves.

Go out and do what you need to do in order to be happy. But only do it if it's what you really want for yourself!

#92 ~ WIIFM

The people we meet throughout our life have not been just sitting around waiting for us to make our grand entrance into their lives. They already have many other interests, a life of their own, so to say. When you first meet new people, you must know that they are not necessarily excited just to be in your presence.

However, I do believe people to be generally hopeful. They are hopeful that, with your arrival, you will have brought along something for them. The idea of *WIIFM*, or **What's In It For Me**, is not quite as self-centered and selfish as it might seem at first. It is, however, the anthem of the busy, and it is the motto of the successful. It is also the question on the conscious or subconscious minds of most, if not all the people you will encounter.

Having a general sense of a person's expectations up front gives you the advantage. Unspoken expectations are the root cause of many arguments, disappointments, failures, and firings. Just knowing from what perspective others are approaching your very first exchange gives you the advantage. It gives you the opportunity to meet or exceed those unspoken expectations.

You have the power of understood expectations on your side just by knowing up front that the people you meet will primarily want to know WIIFM.

So what are you waiting for? Go ahead and tell them. Go ahead and show them!

#93 ~ Count Your Blessings

Count your blessings? Yes, I posed that idea as a question on purpose. That is because the concept of needing to count seems a bit off center given the nature of the many gifts that bless our lives. Why should we need to count them, our blessings, that is? Is it a game? Does the person with the most blessings in life win, or does the person who knows enough to appreciate the gifts wrought of their success end up as the winner?

Can one blessing trump a hundred blessings? Perhaps with a hundred blessings it would be easy to look past the good fortune found within any single blessing, and forget what it means to truly be blessed.

Maybe if you think about it, success is not found in the number of our blessings but in one's ability to see our gifts for the blessing that they are. Maybe it is the realization that we are blessed that turns out to be the greatest blessing of all.

Imagine the potential sadness of your life if you lived in ignorance of all the blessings that your success has made possible.

#94 ~ Embrace Life

Have you ever reached out to hug someone you were glad to see and did not get the sense that they had hugged you back? I have found that when you actively reach out and embrace what life has to offer, you will never be left with such a half-empty feeling. You should know that for those who truly embrace life, their world is always at least half-full.

Full of friends . . .
Full of love . . .
Full of admiration . . .
Full of hope . . .
Full of desire . . .
Full of what today has to offer . . .

Those who reach out to embrace their lives are seldom left holding on to that half-empty feeling. When you see the cup of life as always at least half-full, success, joy, and fulfillment are always within reach.

Nothing fails to be possible because everything is possible when you embrace living. So reach out to those you love. Extend a hand to those with whom you live and work and those people whom you may only have just met. Share with them your passion for living. I promise that when you do, life will return your kindness and hug you back.

#95 ~ Truth Hurts

The truth can hurt but not in the same way in which you can be hurt both short and long term by your failure to actively seek the truth.

Only by seeking out input and honest feedback from those around you can you begin to see clearly your true strengths and real weaknesses.

Understand, not just anyone can help you to see yourself for who you really are. Only those people who care for you, love you, and are concerned for your well-being and happiness are likely to have the courage to tell you the truth.

It is not that the truth is always going to be pleasant to hear, but the truth cannot hurt you. That is because it is the truth, and the truth alone, that sets you free. Only the truth allows you to clearly know the direction you must travel in order to be free to seek and find the happiness you deserve.

#96 ~ It's What You Believe

Go ahead and have an opinion, a personal well-thought-out opinion. You are entitled to have one, though I am not saying that you should share or that you must share that opinion. I am just saying that you should have an opinion.

It is important for you to know what you believe, know why you believe it, and be prepared to justify your beliefs!

Like the words from Kenny Rogers hit song, "The Gambler," "You've got to know when to hold 'em, know when to fold 'em."

Knowing when to hold 'em or when it's best to keep your opinions to yourself can make a big difference in how you are perceived by others. Just because you have an opinion does not mean others want to hear it.

In fact, it might actually be true that the less eager you are to share your opinion, the more likely others will be inclined to seek you out for that opinion, and the more likely it is to be valued when you share with others what you think.

A strong set of beliefs may occasionally be helpful to others should they request your council. However, that same strong set of beliefs is invaluable, as they will most certainly serve as a guide to your everyday choices along the road to your own success.

#97 ~ Soar with Your Strengths

I will tell you a secret many people do not know or never had the opportunity to discover. When you accept or are assigned the position as leader, it often includes the responsibility to delegate tasks in the pursuit of your group goals. Now that, in and of itself, is not the secret. The secret is that this responsibility gives you the opportunity to assign yourself the tasks that you are good at and you enjoy doing.

I first realized the hidden advantages of leadership when I was in business school. Years later, many years later, when reading the book *Soar with Your Strengths* by Donald O. Clifton and Paula Nelson, I received confirmation that seeking out life's opportunities to lead had its own rewards. Over the years, by following this philosophy, I have been able to, as the book title suggests, soar with my strengths.

One day you will be responsible for building your own team, and you will find your greatest chance to be successful in your ability to evaluate your people and their talents. By letting them play the role that allows them to do what they each do best, you allow them to soar with their strengths. This way, you get the most from them as individuals in order to provide the greatest benefit to the team. While at the same time, you still get to assign yourself those tasks you enjoy doing most and are best at doing.

#98 ~ Agony of Victory

Before there was ESPN, the NFL Channel, or pay-per-view, there was ABC Television's *Wide World of Sports*. Every Saturday afternoon, ABC television took you around the world of sports to the big games, big fights, and special events.

To many of that era, the one thing most memorable about the show was that famous line from the show's introduction where they touted, "Thrill of victory and the agony of defeat."

Of course, we all believe that winning is certainly better than losing. However, only after you experience the pride earned within the struggle to reach your goal, will you fully understand the thrill of which ABC spoke. That true thrill found within victory does not exist for those who succeed without the agony of the struggle. That is true because it is only within your hard work, sacrifice, and relentless commitment to conquer a challenge that winning can bring you the personal joy that they refer to as the *thrill of victory*.

Know that there is always going to be an agony in doing the things necessary in order to help one to achieve that kind of hard-fought victory. You will feel it in the agony of getting up early, working late, and always following through.

However, I promise you one thing, the agony of the struggle to succeed will surely pale in comparison to the real personal pain to be found in the *agony of defeat*.

#99 ~ Pay Your Dues

My dad's mom first told me that in order to get to where you want to go, "You've got to pay your dues." Unfortunately, my grandmother died before I could get her to define for me the answer to my $64,000 question . . . *For just how long?*

How long must one pay their dues is the question that has literally haunted me my whole life. I feel like I am paying my dues over and over and over again. It's like in Bill Murray's movie *Groundhog Day*, where every day when he awoke, he had Groundhog Day to live over. Each day he learned new lessons. Each day he developed new skills and new relationships until in the end, he finally got his life right.

That is maybe the way it is supposed to be. Nevertheless, when Grandma talked about the necessity for me to be willing to pay my dues, at the time, I had the distinct feeling that this process was supposed to be a one-and-done kind of thing, like that of paying for a parking ticket. Okay now, I have paid my dues, so let us get on with it. I never imagined it to be the same idea as the need to pay tolls on the Illinois tollway. That is a process where you pay, you pay, and you pay again.

But then again, maybe we are supposed to live life as Bill Murray did in his silly movie, learning and relearning life's lessons until we finally get it right.

So follow Grandma's advice and be willing each day to go out and pay your dues until the success you seek appears miraculously at hand.

#100 ~ Radioactive Confidence

There is a difference between being confident and radiating confidence. Confidence, held close, provides us a comfortable sense of security. However, the personal confidence of those who consistently succeed has an energy all its own. Their personal confidence literally radiates from them, felt by all those with whom they come in contact.

This is the kind of energy that you will find has the power to move mountains. It is only this kind of powerful energy, found in individuals with the highest levels of personal confidence, which can help them to persevere no matter their challenge.

Our personal confidence is the rock upon which we build our life's greatest accomplishments. This rock of personal confidence is the cornerstone of success, yours, mine, and everyone's success.

When you possess such confidence, it will influence the dynamics of your relationships in many unimaginable ways, each of which will result in something new, different, and better!

#101 - Believe in Magic

I believe in magic, not the kind of magic that comes from mystical, magical words like *Abracadabra*. I am talking about those magical words from your childhood that helped you to get that new bike or an extra dessert after eating all your dinner.

I think it is important to remind you that the words *please* and *thank you* have not lost their magical powers. In fact, in today's world of *expect and get*, they can be even more powerful than ever in helping you gain the success you seek.

Please still carries the power to open almost any door in your path. Thank you still has the power to help keep that door open for the next time you need to knock. Both those words reflect our respect and our appreciation to the people with the abilities that can help us to achieve our goals.

You may be lucky enough to receive a favor or an advantage without the power of please. However, you will seldom be reoffered such without the power of appreciation shown by simply saying the thank you.

A well-remembered please may unlock an opportunity to succeed while a sincere thank you has the power to keep that door open for the next time you need pass this way.

Do you believe in magic?

#102 ~ Act Sorry

To say you are sorry and then to fail to change your behavior is a contradiction of fact. The two words *I'm sorry* can have a great deal of power. Successful people understand such power but are smart enough only to use those words when the sentiment matches their intent to change.

We have all heard it said that it takes a big person to say they are sorry. The reality is that anyone at any time can say that they are sorry. It however, does take a person of integrity to say they are sorry with a committed intent to change the behavior for which they have felt the need to apologize.

Saying you're sorry may be the right thing to do but only when you intend to do what it takes to make it right and more importantly, are committed to never allow it to happen again.

#103 ~ Be Like Noah

You know one day in your life it is going to start to rain and rain and rain. Noah was prepared for his forty days and forty nights of rain. Will you be?

I am not suggesting that you start building an ark and collecting animals. What I am suggesting is that the rain represents the unplanned adversity that life invariably brings your way. Just because the specifics of the adversity are unforeseen does not mean that you cannot prepare for when the rains in your life start to fall.

The loss of job, contracting a disease, or acquiring a disability can all make the forty days and forty nights seem like nothing more than a spring shower. So, although the motto *be prepared* belongs to the Boy Scouts, you need to adopt it as your own in order to be ready for the rain.

Saving money for the future, both the one you hope and plan for and the one that may come without warning, is the only way you can even begin to be prepared. Various insurances and a sustainable lifestyle that is within your means may be several additional examples of the measures you should carefully consider when you hope to stay dry.

There is no specific advice for me to offer you or anyone else here. Nevertheless, I can assure you that my personal experience has taught me that you really do not want to get wet.

#104 ~ Something for Nothing

Some say that in life, you should not expect to get *something for nothing*. However, I guess that depends on how you define something and how you define nothing.

Something, when defined as financial success, can come with little or no effort when mixed with a bit of luck. People who win the lottery find the highest levels of financial success on a very small cash investment. In this case, I am sure we could agree that they have gotten something for nothing.

Yet this quick-fix methodology of finding your life's success through nothing more than a lightning strike of luck is, at best, a poor bet on anyone's part.

I suggest that you do not count on or hope for a lightning strike of luck when looking for your success in life. The success you seek will be worth so much more when you have been willing to pay for it through the cost of your personal efforts to make it happen.

#105 ~ Nothing to Fear

In President Franklin D. Roosevelt's 1933 inaugural address, he was quoted as saying, "We have nothing to fear but fear itself."

I believe that self-confidence is nothing more than the absence of personal fear as it relates to our own life. Self-confidence endeavors to quiet that internal voice of fear that incessantly works to persuade us that it *can't be done*. It is only through our internal confidence in ourselves that we have the power to wrestle back control of our heart and mind from the grips of fear.

I'm afraid are two words that, when allowed to slip into our conscious thought, can become justification for and a guarantee of future failure.

Roosevelt declared fear as the enemy of his nation, going on to say that fear is a "nameless, unreasoning, unjustified terror which paralyzes needed efforts to convert retreat into advance."

When you look at the real risk of heeding to your fears, it is not in taking the chance and failing or making the leap and falling. The real risk of letting your fears control your actions is in allowing those fears to keep you from reaching out for your goals at all.

#106 ~ Know the Height of the Bar

Your ability to exceed the expectations of those who you serve is possible through your ongoing efforts to clarify their expectations.

Remember, those who work to deliver more than is expected are often repaid for more than they have delivered. It is this *just a bit more* philosophy that has the power to change the dynamics between people.

Knowing this, it is incumbent on you and your efforts to be successful to clearly understand what specifically others expect of you. You can make no excuse for your failure to do so since I have told you that the cost for ignoring this simple fact is too high to pay.

You can start down your own road to success by clarifying the expectations of all those around you by directly asking them, "How high is the bar?" Then you only need to be patient and attentive as you listen to what they have to tell you.

#107 ~ Common Sense . . . Nonsense

Somewhere along the line, I am pretty sure, you have had someone tell you, "That's just common sense." My guess is that we have all heard those words before from parents, friends, or a boss. My thought for you here is to tell you that there is no such thing as common sense. If common sense were actually common, then why wouldn't we all have it? If we did all have the same common sense, then we would all act in the same, common sense manner under similar circumstances.

Now you could argue that it is common sense to put a coat on when cold. People also say that it is common sense for you to get food when you are hungry. However, these common responses are as instinctual as pulling your hand from a hot stovetop.

Even though individual responses to each of these situations can be said to have a high degree of commonality, the same cannot be said about how we all react to most of life's other challenges.

So look to develop and depend on your own level of *uncommon sense*. With that level of considered judgment, you will be able to successfully navigate any obstacle course life sets in your path.

Common sense to one person is nonsense to another. Look carefully for the answers that will work best for you. With that said, I would suggest that I hope you have the common sense to pull your hand from atop the hot stove!

#108 ~ It's a Marathon

Life is a marathon of billions of steps toward your most significant goals. However, life's marathon differs from that of the road race. Life's journey of one foot placed in front of the other is not limited to steps that only move you forward. If that were so, then anyone could successfully run the race.

It is life's two steps forward and the inevitable one step back that throws so many people off their balance.

It is life's largest failures and its smallest disappointments that have the potential to throw us off our rhythm. Yet to succeed, we must guard against these efforts to take away our momentum by distorting our focus and commitment to the journey.

You should consider the inevitable step back to be nothing more than the single step that precedes your next step forward.

#109 ~ Confident Ignorance

Profit and *loss* are words that seem to be so contrary. Yet it is only though your attempts to profit from your mistakes that you obtain the ability to turn your personal ship, *Titanic*, before you become victim to the iceberg.

This means that within every lost opportunity, there is another opportunity to find a true blessing in disguise.

However, there is a difference between making note of a mistake and implementing a solution to avoid it the next time. When you say you have learned a lesson, yet you fail to change your behavior, you obviously have not learned the lesson.

If all that I am saying is true, then knowledge without change is nothing more than *confident ignorance.*

#110 ~ Stand Out

Within any given industry, as within life in general, products of similar nature compete for their place within the conscious minds of customers. Yet many times, even the most educated consumer can find little difference upon which to base his/her decision to buy a product or buy into an idea.

This decision often then falls to the fact that the singular difference of measure may end up being you!

Therefore, give the people around you a clear sense of who you are. Help them to feel comfortable enough about you that they feel confident in forgoing the complicated and mundane process of analysis in order to move forward. All this can happen based solely on their perception of who they believe you to be as a person.

So make an effort to share yourself, and you will be able to connect with others on a personal level. You really need to let them know who you are. For when you do, they most certainly will choose to do business with you and be part of your life.

I guess this is proof again that all aspects of life are simply selling!

#111 ~ Work Your Plan

Success does not always have to seem to be just out of reach. It does not always have to come as a struggle. When you know what you want, such as having a clearly defined vision for your future, you are halfway home to reaching your goals. It is only through this clarified vision of your final destination, knowing precisely what you need to achieve, that makes your accomplishment of this level of success possible and probable.

It is the process by which you establish your goal or goals that defines for you the first step toward fulfillment. By possessing a vision of the final desired result, you can easily lay in place a plan to take you the rest of the way home.

It is the very process of planning for your success that will set you apart, and in the end, that planning will put you into position successfully to complete your journey.

#112 ~ Tortoise and the Hare

We do not define the beauty of a rose by the number of blooms on a single bush, but rather, we define its beauty by the delicate elegance of a single bloom seen through an appreciative eye.

Similarly, when building a career, do not get caught up measuring your success by the quantity of your accomplishments over a short length of time. Rather, measure your success by the quality of each experience in and of itself.

Doing the right things over time will give you the right results. Maybe what we are talking about here is the lesson learned from the story of the tortoise and the hare. This is where we first discovered that slow and steady wins the race.

Yet, I am not suggesting slow as the key to building a career. What I am saying is that the consistency, as prescribed by the steady, is what will most certainly create the positive results you seek over the long road you will travel.

#113 ~ Multi-tasking Myth

Of course, you can walk and chew gum at the same time. Yet it is from your seemingly miraculous ability to execute these two such mentally undemanding tasks simultaneously that society has concluded that multi-tasking is the road to higher levels of personal productivity at every level.

However, our ability to perform any simple task while doing another is not proof that multitasking will bring us the holy grail of extra time and greater success.

The power of focus does not equally mislead us. For example, when you focus the sun's light through a magnifying glass, you create energy enough to generate fire.

It is only by focusing your own personal energy on the successful completion of a single task that will ignite the fire of your own accomplishment.

#114 ~ It's in You

I believe that a person's joy for life is visible to others through their smile. You see, it is through our smiles and our laughter that we are able to externalize the joy we have in our lives.

However, before you can radiate your true inner beauty, you must first discover and appreciate the beauty of living the life that is all around you. Only then, when you have internalized all of what life offers as part of the person that you are, will the inner-you come shining through. It is in this moment that everyone can see that your joy for life is what sparks your smile.

While that may be true, I also believe that your smile is also joy's gateway into your heart. Smile and let in the joy that each day has to offer.

This means you should laugh a little and let in the joy. Smile a little and let in the joy. Think about it, how can anyone filled with joy help but radiate an inner beauty for all to see?

#115 ~ It's About Time

When did life get so busy that everything we do and how we value it is in some way related to the time it will take to finish that task?

You too, in your journey to become successful, need to evaluate your activities in terms of their *return on investment*. For the time being, you will closely have to measure your investment of your time in order to define that the completion of the task is a success.

This process of constant evaluation has almost become mandatory if you are to establish any degree of balance in your life. That is because today, most people do not go home when their work is finished; they go home when they are tired. So many jobs are really nothing more than the day-to-day continuation of an ongoing process with no specific ending point.

How do you get it down to basics? How do you really decide what should be your specific return on investment for the effort you put in? Well, that is something you are going to have to answer for yourself. But what I do hope I can relay to you is that in order to get what you want, you have to first decide what you are willing to give up in order to get it.

The lesson we must all understand is that you cannot do it all, and nothing worthwhile comes without a cost. So seek to know specifically, what are you willing to invest in order to get that which you desire?

#116 ~ Meaning of a Word

How can a word carry so much baggage?

How can a word carry such a high level of negativity?

If you say, "I have a problem," your first response may be, "Oh, Oh!" Yet when confronted by a *challenge,* many individuals reposition themselves in order to focus their energies differently and work to create a solution.

The issue of concern may be the same, but I believe your outlook and your internal talk is substantially different when confronted by a problem than when life presents you with a challenge.

To ensure you maintain the attitude necessary to reach your goals, never define any challenge to your success as a problem that you need to overcome. Challenge implies a solution is possible. We face challenges with hope. We often see a problem as a hopeless dead end. Call it semantics if you want, but I think it's effect is more powerful than that.

Take the challenges that life presents and leave its problems for others to deal with.

#117 ~ Dumb Blonde

If ever there were ever two words that clearly define the essence of stereotyping, they are the words *dumb blonde.* I know that you would certainly agree with this statement.

"What do you call a blonde professor?"

"Nothing, it was a trick question. That's because it could never happen!"

In the end, the punch lines may vary.

Are they stupid? Yes!

Are they a clear definition of stereotyping? Yes!

Are they thoughtless and hurtful? Yes!

What stereotype do you project by your race, creed, or gender? What stereotypes do you apply by others' behaviors based on their degree, their appearance, or place of origin?

Jokes that play on society's stereotypes are never truly funny. Nevertheless, they should act as powerful reminders to each of us in search of success. That is, some people only see us through the distortion of the stereotypes they use to define us. While at the same time, we need to be aware that we too may unfairly judge others through similar distorted stereotypes.

Being aware of the negative power of your own views is the first step in helping others to see you, as you want to be seen.

#118 ~ K~I~S~S

Often, our success best can be achieved through our ability to communicate our ideas. I believe that in business, as in life, the number one reason people hear the word *no* is simply that the people with whom you are dealing just do not clearly understand what they are being asked. They do not have the time to consider your point because they are confused about what you are asking of them. In fact, they are so confused that they just do not even want to think about it and they do not want to put in the effort to figure it out, so their answer is, "No!"

To be successful, you need to learn to cut through the mental clutter and pressure of one's daily life. You need to focus your message, and you need to keep things simple. When I say simplicity, you might want to read the word *clarity*. Keeping it clear makes understanding your thoughts easier.

When people are confused, they are often more likely not to trust. If it is complicated, they believe that they must be extra careful so as not to end up taken advantage of.

The mind of those you hope to persuade fears that which it does not understand. Keeping it clear may mean keeping your presentation simple by breaking up your ideas into bite-size thoughts that do not require lengthy consideration. If you want to reach through all the distractions that keep you from communicating your ideas effectively, then the answer is to **Keep It Simple, Stupid.**

#119 ~ Love the One You're With

When you are looking to develop successful long-term personal or business relationships, you will be most successful when you singularly focus on those individuals as people when you are with them.

There is a great hook line from a 1970s rock song. "If you can't be with the one you love, love the one you're with." Now that advice may certainly be suspect as it applies to the development of your long-term love interests. Yet, the advice is spot on when applied to the development of long-term personal and business relationships.

You see, in order to truly connect to people, you need to personally reach out to the people you are with at that moment. Your personal commitment and attentiveness is a key to the development of any relationship. If the people around you are important enough to spend your time with, then they are important enough to give your full attention to while you are together.

You may be prone to multi-task in many areas of your life. Nevertheless, to build successful relationships, you must stay focused and not try to multi-task your way through this effort.

All you have to do is love the ones you are with, and they might just love you back!

#120 ~ New Ideas

"You are open to new ideas, aren't you?" I think that is a truly great selling line. Who can possibly answer that question by saying no and still look like an intelligent individual?

However, this question has even greater power in helping you find the success that you seek. To find success as an individual, you must remain open to new ideas. I am not suggesting your ideals flap in the social winds of change. However, I am saying that you should be open to the new ideas presented you.

You have to wonder how certain individuals can be so sure that they are right all the time. They act certain that they have the right answers and purposely block out all contrary information in a display of *ideological bigotry*. They purposefully turn their backs on important information that has the potential to open their eyes to different points of view about important issues.

"Sticks and stones may break my bones, but words will never hurt me!" If that is true, then what do people really fear from the different combination of words that, when brought together, make up a new idea? What are they really afraid of?

I submit to you that if you are not open to different ideas, then you cannot possibly expect to grow and evolve into the person you need to one day become.

#121 ~ No Pain, No Gain

Think for a second. What are the accomplishments in your life of which you are most proud? Were they the things that came easily for you? Most likely, the accomplishments of which you are most proud are the ones that you only achieved through challenge and struggle.

Great things rise from great struggle. This fact should give you confidence next time you find yourself challenged. You can know that if you persevere, something great could just happen. Your struggle can mean that success is getting so close that you can almost taste it. That alone should give you the incentive to continue fighting the battle to move forward.

No pain, no gain was the physical fitness battle cry of the 1980s. People's belief in that single statement gave millions the confidence to push through the pain toward their goals . . . or should I say, pulled muscles.

I am not saying that you will always find success at the end of long and painful journeys. What I am telling you is that you need to be prepared in life to fight for what you want. What I am telling you is that your ultimate success is the light that you will eventually see at the end of the tunnel.

#122 ~ Put the Ball in Play

Yes, with each breath you draw, you prepare for life's next sale. This is true for all of us, not just those who we label as salespeople.

We prepare . . . to sell our kids on doing their homework.

We prepare . . . to sell our spouse on going out for dinner.

We prepare . . . to sell our boss on giving us a raise.

Right in the middle of dinner, you prepare to sell yourself on the necessity of indulging your sweet tooth, even though you are currently in the middle of your diet.

Now I know there is certainly a difference between those who sell and those who close sales. This point of difference is clearly the definition of what is effective selling activity versus just engaging in the activity of selling.

I clearly then connect your successful ability to sell to your eventual success in life. To sell is, in essence, to breathe. One cannot happen without the other.

How then can you become more successful in your life as a whole? The answer is to become more successful at selling yourself. Not everyone will make every sale. The difference is in the batting average of the big hitters versus the utility infielders.

It is clear that big-league success will come from your ability to occasionally hit the home-run and to find new ways every day to put the ball in play in order to achieve your goals.

#123 ~ Room for Improvement

Each of us is blessed in life with various strengths and often less than blessed with corresponding weaknesses. I know you want to be the best you can be. Therefore, with limited resources, the question you must then ask is, "Do you accomplish this more quickly by polishing strengths or by striving to overcome weaknesses?"

Few of us, no, none of us, can say that we have no room for improvement. Yet it seems obvious that you will find more potential growth by putting away the polishing cloth you use to hone your strengths and get right down to the more demanding job of building up your weaknesses. Improvement here can bring exponential opportunities for growth.

However, when we get out the polishing cloth, we are able to refine our strengths in order to help us achieve a level of excellence, and it's that level of excellence that allows us to stand out as individuals. When you make what you are good at, something you are great at, you give yourself your best chance to find the success you are looking for.

Hold it! Which is the right answer? My answer to you is that it doesn't matter in which direction you travel. You can claim exponential growth through turning a weakness into strength. While on the other hand, you can also claim success by turning your strengths into skills that allow you to stand out above the rest.

There is no right answer, except to say that both options require an individual's commitment to grow as a person. In both cases, the status quo takes a backseat to an individual's desire to get better. My advice is to harness that desire to improve in whichever direction you desire, and your ultimate success will be the final result.

#124 ~ Surprise

Yes, you have heard me, and pretty much everyone else expound on the virtues of setting and striving for your life's goals. Oops! The others and I may have overstated the case for focusing on goal setting. Yes, I did write that here!

Even though I know the truth, I may have previously failed to articulate that which is without doubt the most important personality trait in realizing your success. *Spontaneity!* The fact is you will likely find more joy by going along with those many experiences that arrive unplanned, thus taking us all by surprise.

Yes, you may have charted your trip through life, marking each road and circling each planned stop. You have made sure that your goals are clear. You have decided both your method for reaching your goal as well as the route you will take to get there.

Yet the greatest experiences in life can be the ones we never planned for or expected. These opportunities present themselves out of your planned sequence, and in a mere moment, you must decide whether to deviate from the plan, let loose, and really experience life, or go with the plan.

It would seem, based on commonly held beliefs, that the act of goal setting and planning for your life and success is a key factor in getting all the things you ever dreamed of or wanted. Nevertheless, in reality, it is just as important that you trust your *sense of opportunity.* It is in those unforeseen moments that have the potential to get you all the things you never believed were possible!

#125 ~ R~E~S~P~E~C~T

We live our lives, each and every day, in hope that our friends, family, and coworkers will realize an appreciation of our skills. We seek nothing more than respect for who we are, for our ideas, and for our role in the success of the overall group.

Comedian Rodney Dangerfield made a career of his famous line, "I don't get no respect." The rest of us also find that our lives require our own very similar quest for a level of personal respect. Bottom line is that we all just want others to appreciate us.

Successful individuals start their quest for that elusive respect by first respecting themselves. I would go so far as to say that you could never reach even one of your life goals until you respect the person who you see in the mirror each day.

Do you respect the people around you who do not respect themselves? In the end, self-respect is the primer to self-confidence. I ask you, who can respect an individual who does not respect him or herself? Further, how do you respect that person if they lack the self-confidence even to stand up for what they believe?

Respect the person you see in the mirror each morning because he/she has worked hard to earn your appreciation.

#126 ~ Blowin' in the Wind

The winds of change are always blowing. However, the word *change* in and of itself does nothing to clarify the value of the action defined as change. Whether it is change for the better or change for the worse, we define both situations simply as change.

Ask yourself, which way are the winds in your life blowing? Are you better off to let those winds of change take you with them, or should you struggle forward against prevailing opinions into the teeth of the biting winds of change?

This advice is not so much to tell you that one choice is superior to the other. I only want to let you know that every once in a while, you should wet your finger and hold it up to judge the direction of shifting winds.

Every situation is different. Yet knowing which way the winds of change blow may carry you halfway to your destination with little or no effort.

#127 ~ Silence is Golden

Music that moves us emotionally does not do so based on its predictability. Musicians achieve this connection with their listeners not by doing what is expected. They make the connection by putting notes together with a musicality that never before has been experienced.

Yet at the same time, nothing may have more power to move us than a well-placed moment of silence between the voices of opposing notes. It is clear that the silence has power to draw us in like no other combination of notes.

Our voice and the words we use have the same power to move people. This is when we consciously work to create a flow of words or ideas that are effectively broken and given emphasis by moments of well-placed silence. Silence gives people a chance to reflect. This break in the action stands clearly apart from what came before or will come after. More than any single word, the lack of a word and the silence that replaces it, act as an exclamation point to your effort to communicate successfully.

The words you choose affect your ability to communicate. However, powerful communication probably is affected most by the words you choose to leave unsaid.

#128 ~ How to Get There

The idea that the *end justifies the means* is a core belief of those literally willing to do *whatever it takes* to get what they want. However, when you hear me tout the importance of being willing to do whatever it takes to achieve success, I assure you I do not mean you should ignore the means by which you choose to reach your end.

The difference between the two is that the validity of your end goal—your success as it were—is only to be valued if the road you hope to travel to get there is the high one. Think first of who you are and how you want others to see you when you chart your course to success. If you find that the things you must do to reach your goals are not representative of the person you really are, then it should be clear that the end does not justify the means.

To justify the road to your goals in the face of what you must sacrifice in terms of your personal integrity is to miss the true meaning of the word *success*. You can start by defining the parameters for your own success simply as the necessity for you to stay true to yourself and your beliefs in whatever you do. This way, you allow yourself to maintain your self-respect in your active pursuit of all that you dream.

#129 ~ Going in First

I was watching one time as three young kids came to the edge of the pool. One asked the others, "Who's going in first?" "Not me!" said a second. "I will," said the third as he boldly stepped toward the water's edge. Then in a moment of hesitation, he stopped short. Turning to the other two, he said, "I'll go if you guys go."

There they stood, three kids in swimsuits ready to swim. No one was willing to dive in first, so nothing happened. The opportunity of the moment was lost to individual and group indecisiveness.

Have you ever found yourself at a pool's edge, afraid to take the leap? You know, jump in with both feet or take the dive? Are you the kind of person who dips a toe prior to experiencing each of life's opportunities?

Maybe from time to time, it is prudent to dip a toe. Yet if others see the dipping as hesitation and/or fear, then maybe your caution has gone beyond prudence. I am not saying or suggesting that you blindly leap without consideration, for that could be reckless, as the water could be very cold.

What I am saying is that you will never win the race if you stand by the side of the pool watching as your friends swim away.

#130 ~ Ya' Gonna' Pay

When you find that your life is a lot more about *give* than *take*, you will have to be willing to take the consequences of your givin' it! Even the most avid partygoers cannot give it all the time. That is because you will not find success in the wee hours of the morning. That is, unless the purpose for finding yourself up and out or bed during those wee hours is to get a jump on your competition.

Now that you are older, it has to be hard to remember waking up every morning without a care in the world. However, there was a time when the idea that *I'll get to it tomorrow* was really good enough for now. It was a time when your responsibilities were easily set aside or forgotten. It makes you wonder, *what can a day hurt, when your entire life stretches out before you?*

There is usually a price to be paid by those who play too much. The price is different for everyone. Generally, I would say the result of attempting to burn a candle at both ends usually leaves many of those who attempt to do so with burns on both sides of their fingers.

Of course, you should play and play hard. Play as much as you can because life is too short for all this to be about nothing but work.

Just never lose sight of your real goals because you will end up nodding off, completely exhausted when the rest of the world is out there grabbing for your brass ring.

#131 ~ Ya' Gotta Wanna'

Love, money, friends. If you do not want it all bad enough, you are not likely to get all you hope for from life. Success by any definition requires a person to reach out boldly and grab for the elusive brass ring.

Maybe what I am talking about is having a *can do* attitude. No, I am not suggesting that you need to run up the backs of those around you. I am suggesting that you won't likely end up first in anything unless you are willing to put yourself personally on the line to get it. It's as they say, "Ya' gotta wanna'!"

The question that maybe you need to answer first is, *Would you be satisfied with having to settle for less than you know is possible?* Only through your willingness to struggle through—in order to get what you want—will you have any other option.

So what then defines proper aggressiveness? Well, I do not think it is about being physical, and I know it is not about being rude. I think that it might be politically correct to define proper aggressiveness as being *consistently persistent.*

Of course, at some point, we all need to take no for an answer. If this statement is true, then know that if you want to be successful, you certainly cannot afford to take the first no that comes your way.

So put your head down, and with the right attitude, go aggressively after the things you want and need in order for yourself to feel successful.

#132 ~ Don't Fall Off

Sometimes a person has to push themself to their limit, to the very edge in order to find success. In the end, it is not about how hard or how far you have to go in order to reach your goals. It is only about whether or not you have the courage and stamina to take it all the way there.

When all seems dark and hopes for success seem dim, there are those who will push themselves through the challenges before them in order to earn their prize. That is how you differentiate between those individuals likely to succeed and those most likely to fail. We see failure, in this example, as just a lack of willingness by a person to risk success.

It is not always easy to fight through, not everyone is willing to pay the cost. People naturally fear the risks that present themselves in their effort to take one last shot. However, to succeed, they must take their quest to the very edge of their abilities, to the very edge of their convictions.

Imagine those first minutes with Columbus when, in front of him, he only saw water, and behind him, he watched as the land he knew disappeared from sight. He was willing to take his quest to the very edge in order to prove that the world was not flat.

How far are you willing to go to prove your world is not flat? Are you willing to take it all the way to the edge?

#133 ~ Roll Over

A dog may be the smartest animal alive. As a dog, it knows that in order to get what it wants, all it has to do is ask. People have wants and needs, and yet they almost seem afraid to articulate them. A dog wants his belly scratched, and all he needs to do is roll over and look straight at you until you bend over and scratch his belly.

It is the confidence he has when he rolls over that allows him to achieve his immediate goal of having a belly rub. You can see the confidence in his eyes as he lays his expectation out for the world to see.

What is it that you want so badly that you are willing to risk allowing everyone to know your hopes and expectations? How is it that you think you can get what you want from life if you do not have the courage to ask or simply to tell the world what it is you want?

The dog is not afraid to let his expectations be known by all, and he gets what he wants by staring you down. A dog never breaks eye contact until he realizes his goal.

So roll over and let the world know what you expect from it. Just make sure that you are not the first one to blink.

#134 ~ You Can't Be Certain

The next time you find yourself in a disagreement with your friends, family, or coworkers, I would like to suggest to you that there is a 66.6666666 percent probability that you are wrong.

Here is why that is true. If you and I disagree, there are only three possible scenarios as to who is right. The first is that you are right, and I am wrong. The second scenario is just the opposite, with you being wrong and me being right. The third and final possibility is that we are both wrong, which is the only other option because we certainly both cannot be right.

That is it; in two of the three situations described above, I was wrong. In two of the three scenarios, you were wrong. This simple explanation allows us all to understand the fact that whenever we find ourselves in a situation where we disagree with someone, the probability is that we are wrong.

Successful people know how to admit when they are wrong. Successful people know the odds, and they know that they most likely will be wrong more often than they will be right. So look at each disagreement as an opportunity to gain new information. This new information may provide you a different perspective regarding the subject at hand, and it will certainly give you the perfect chance to admit to the world that you were wrong.

#135 ~ There Will Be Challenges

What is the difference between an inconvenience and a challenge? Some might say it is all a matter of degree, while others might suggest that it is all a matter of perspective.

I say that no matter how you define the word, those things that we today see to be a challenge would be nothing more than a minor inconvenience to our ancestors. The pioneering spirit of our ancestors allowed them to keep heading west in the face of *insurmountable inconveniences.*

They were not turned back because the train was late . . . There was no train!

They were not deterred just because that night there was nothing for dinner . . . There often was no dinner!

They were not beaten back because they had to work overtime . . . They just worked all the time!

What is it that challenges you? What is it that you define as mere inconvenience? Just by your definition of the words, your perspective tilts one way or the other. Of course, we all can endure a little inconvenience. That is not my concern. The more important question to me is, "Are you up for the challenge?"

#136 ~ I Can't Hear You

Annoying . . . that sound is nothing but annoying! That is why the squeaky wheel gets the grease. It is there, always there, telling you what it wants, what it wants, what it wants. More importantly though, it is there consistently telling you what it needs.

I would suggest that you consider the squeaky wheel to be the world's finest definition of *persistent persuasion*. Well, on second thought, maybe you would have to consider the endless whining of a two-year-old to be a close contender. The point is that the process of persuasion in both these cases is based on a constant, consistent, and clearly heard message.

What must you do so that those around you will be able to understand what it is you want or what it is you need in order to reach your goals? When your goal is to have your voice heard, then being ignored is never an option. That is why I suggest that you learn to be the squeaky wheel!

#137 ~ Speak Up

If you do not take the opportunity to share your ideas, no one will ever know the depth of your creative well. So speak up! There really are people out there waiting to hear what you have to say.

We have all heard of the reference to an individual as the *strong, silent* type. However, we never really hear about that type of person being a leader of anything. Unless that is, you are talking about the talk-softly-and-carry-a-big-stick type of leader like any of actor John Wayne's characters. Generally, strong, silent types find themselves relegated or relegate themselves to the back row. As I see it, it will be those people with passion for their ideas who will eventually find themselves standing front and center, inspiring others and leading the way. That is a very clear indication of a person's strength of conviction.

Where is it that you stand or, should I say, sit? How can you see a person as being a leader when they are seldom ever seen or heard?

I suggest to you that great ideas and their creators are often seen as leaders as they have earned the respect and admiration of all those around them. So stand up in order to stand out.

When you boldly share your ideas with others, you will certainly experience all the opportunities for success that your ideas are worthy of.

#138 ~ Elusive Perfection

Why is everyone always so preoccupied with the concept of perfection?

It is like I've always told you, "You do not need to try and be a perfect person . . . You only need to try to be yourself!"

No one expects perfection from you. Those around you, from your coworkers to significant others, are not expecting perfection. They are only expecting you!

Just like you, those around you will make mistakes. Those mistakes do not make them bad people. You need to realize that making mistakes only makes them people.

You too are a person. By holding yourself to the unattainable standard of perfection, you are denying yourself the opportunity to appreciate the success you already have attained.

#139 ~ Celebrate Your Independence

Who is watching over you? By that, I mean, who is looking out for your best interests? Who is it within your working world that would have your back when the pressure is on and will always be there for you no matter what? The answer is maybe as sad as it is simple. The answer is, no one! Sorry to be jaded, but as my experience has shown me, it will all be up to you if you are to reach your goals.

So begin down your road to success by writing your own Declaration of Independence.

Declare independence from those who control . . .
Declare independence from those who judge . . .
Declare independence from those who are part of the problem and not part of the solution . . .

When I say declare independence, I am not suggesting you turn your back on your boss or on the system. I am suggesting that you just prepare yourself for the fact that if you are to get all that you dream of, you are going to have to be independent enough to get it for yourself.

You cannot look for or rely on other people to pull you up because you will only consider yourself successful when you have pulled yourself up.

#140 ~ Final Word

By now, you should know that you do not measure your success in life by the material things around you. I am talking about the visible things, such as the size of your home, the number of your toys, and the extravagance of your vacations. Leave the fascination of those things to others and turn a blind eye to the people who pronounce your success based upon those shallow measures of a person's worth.

Truly, to know that you have become successful, you must not base your success on what you have or what others say about you. Measure your success only by who it is you have become, that is, the person you see in the mirror. What you see and what is in your heart define for you your true measure of success.

Success might best be defined as your contentment with who you are . . . It is your pride of accomplishment . . . It is your love of and for friends and family . . . In other words, you measure success by your own happiness with who you have become as a person.

Now it is clear. You are the only one who has the ability to define your life as being a success. You are the only one who knows what it is that is inside of you. Yet more than that, you are the only one whose judgment should matter.

View from the Top

*My Final Thoughts about
Achieving Success*

by Kristine's dad

Dear Kristine,

When I last came to visit you in October of 2009, I had told you about the excitement I had experienced the night before I flew out to San Diego. All night long my mind had raced, filled with thoughts regarding the challenges you have taken on out there in California. With the stress of it all, I felt during that time as if I were living it myself, through you. That includes both the steps forward you have taken . . . and, of course, the occasional steps backward. I guess that is natural for a parent.

Mostly, what had my mind racing that night was my out-of-the-blue fixation on something you had said to me just a week before. You shared a story with me. It was a story about how you had decided that, "Successful people *always* do the right thing." I was proud of you as you told me the story of how you had seen the business you worked for, in your opinion, not do the right thing in a particular instance for their customer. You told me how it was clear to you that by not doing the right thing, the cost to your company, in terms of lost future business, had been extremely high. Much higher than if they had just done what was right in the first place. As I considered your words, I knew for certain that so much of what we had talked about over the years had made a permanent impression on the person you've become. Additionally, you had also taken the foundation of your upbringing by your mom and I to formulate a solid philosophy that will guide your decision making for years to come.

There I was, lying in that motel bed with my mind literally bursting with various ideas I hoped to share with you that weekend. Restlessly, I lay there, thinking about your assertion regarding successful people's responsibility to always do the right thing; I just could not turn it all off.

With all that going on in my head, I rolled out of bed and made my way to the desk in the corner of the room. It was somewhat funny to me, the realization that this moment of clarity and creativity came about due to some delayed emotional response to conversation that, until then, I had forgotten. Whatever the cause of all this energy, I felt inspired.

I often roll out of bed to write my thoughts down. When you get to be my age, you just cannot count on remembering things. Then, the next morning when my mind is fresh, I finish them. However, that night, by the light of my BlackBerry, I wrote, and when I had finished, hours had passed, and I had written twenty additional thoughts about finding success.

I hate to admit it, but as of late, these moments of inspiration have been few and far between. Perhaps it is the aging process. Maybe it was the events of the last year and the pressures from the challenge of your mom's cancer. Maybe it was all the thought and discussion surrounding the planning of your sister's wedding. In any event, it seems like it has been a very long time since I last had experienced that level of creative energy.

Looking back, I wonder why I just did not turn on the bedroom light, but I really did not want to wake up. Funny, I know. Once I started writing, one thought flowed into another and another. I kept thinking, this idea is the last one, and then I will crawl back into bed. Well, that just did not play out as planned. As you know, I was so excited about what I had written that night that I shared those thoughts with you right after my plane landed. Looking back, those moments of creative energy just felt magical. It felt so good to be writing again, and I felt so connected, so alive, so useful.

Maybe the bigger question is, why write a third book in the first place? I didn't plan it, but it was during that weekend we spent together when everything came together. At the time, I had finished writing the second book and was certain that it was my last. As you may remember, the last thought I wrote was called the "Final Word." I had really planned to be done. Yet it started again that night in that dark motel room. Maybe I realized in those BlackBerry-lit moments that I had more that I wanted and needed to say to you.

Well, it did not take long for time to clarify my thoughts about a third book. You will remember, the morning after I arrived, we got up early to go hiking at Torrey Pines State Natural Reserve along the Pacific Ocean. As we started our walk up to the top of a coastal ridge, literally, I felt overcome physically by how difficult it seemed. Not even a quarter of the way up the hill half my water bottle was gone, and it was not even hot out. Yes, this is a pretty big hill, but it certainly is no Mount Everest. Quickly, my body made clear to me that it had been a bit too long since I had done any real exercise. It was just so difficult getting started again. Each successive step made me painfully aware of the effort that would be necessary to take the next step. The road, as it winded its way toward the top, just kept on stretching upward. Due to all the curves, I could see no definitive end and had no clue to how long it might take us to reach our end destination. I just wished we could have been done. It was then that it hit me! Our climb that morning was a metaphor for our own personal journeys through life. Sounds dramatic, I know, but keep reading and see if what I'm saying starts to make sense to you.

Firstly, as in any task, it is hard to get started, and many people never even get out of the blocks. Each step upward, our purpose in life, does not come without effort. In order to keep our forward momentum, we must continually struggle. Then on top of all that, we do not know definitively where the road takes us or where it will end. In those brief, mostly out-of-breath moments, I had seen clearly the relevance of everything I had written to you in the past as well as many of the thoughts I hoped to share with you for the future.

Somewhere, just over halfway to the top, my muscles seemed to wake up and remember how to move, and my breathing became much less labored. Seemingly, without any real effort, I began moving forward and upward at an ever-increasing pace. Again, this moment relates to how we reach our goals in life. You see, once you make a commitment, incremental progress is less of a process of start and stop, than it is a process designed to maintain your momentum.

It was at this point that I saw that doing the right thing was no longer a decision for you; it was simply your reaction to the circumstances at hand. The cool thing was—if my beliefs about the true meaning of our climb were correct—your continued growth would be just a natural progression of achieving one goal after another.

I know what you are thinking. How is it that all this stuff is running through your dad's head when we were supposed to be just out for a bit of a walk? That is how it works for me. I never know from where my next inspiration will come from. During times like this, I go with it and let my imagination run. All the while, we just keep walking.

It was about two-thirds of the way to the top when I again noted that our pace had continued to gain speed. We were now actually starting to pass a few people along the way. Yet at the same time, I noticed other people passing us at a pace that propelled them upward at a much faster rate than our own. However, the real clarity about how this experience was just like life came to me as I took notice of the expressions on the faces of each person as they worked their way to the top. No matter if we were passing them, or they were passing us, there was a look of confident determination. I was amazed at the focus reflected on all their faces. The clarity of purpose, found in the faces of those people, revealed to me that life and our effort to succeed is all about our own personal journey to the top.

I can imagine that you still may not be convinced regarding my perception in this matter. At its roots, this entire experience is really how it is in our own life's struggles. All the elements of your own personal journey are here. The path is yours, the pace is yours, and you will, based on your choices, arrive ahead of some and long after others. On your journey up that ladder of success, you also meet people who, for many reasons, are coming down. That is, going in the opposite direction. This morning's adventure really had it all.

It was in these moments of personal reflection regarding the true meaning of our hiking expedition that I again felt a need to help you. Then without notice, we arrived. We had finally reached the end of the road, and now it was our time to take a moment to stop and enjoy our own *view from the top*. We had made it, and together, we took great joy in our reward, a most magnificent view.

As I stood there, wind in my face, I wondered how many people would get to see the view from the top of their own hill. Would they get started, would they persevere, or would they turn back, overwhelmed by the process. As a result, they would end up defeated by the uncertainty of it all, turned back by their realization that their final destination might never be clear until their last step. It is only in that final moment that you actually know that you have arrived, and in arriving, you realize that for today you have succeeded.

As we were later on our way down that hill, I decided that I was now certain that the time had come to write this book—what I felt would certainly be the final edition of my thoughts about finding success. After our little adventure that day, I was again motivated to write, and I now had my title. I would call your third book "View from the Top: My Final Thoughts about Achieving Success."

I am so pleased that I have finally gotten the chance to tell you how our morning together profoundly affected me. It was a good time, and I have enjoyed reliving the experience with you again as an integral part of this final gift to you.

For many, their road to find success is just a walk up the hill. For others—and you are one of those people—the journey to overcome life's challenges and the road that stretches ahead of you is an adventure waiting to be lived. What inspires me is that you see each step that you take as a challenge and each step forward as a victory. As you read what I have written here for you, I remind you of the fact that "you inspire me to be better than I really am."

Love always,

Dad

Contents: View from the Top

#141 ~ The Joy is in the Moment

Sure, you must look ahead and plan in order to be successful, and it is certainly necessary that you must be able to look back in order to learn from past experience in order to grow.

However, you need to know that real success . . . true joy of life is found in this very moment. When you are in the moment, it is real, and it is now!

If you let it, you can define your success by the joy you experience through the people you are with, the place that you are at, and the road you are on right now!

Do not look back and do not look forward—to be in the moment, you need only look around!

#142 ~ The Power to Create

I am not the world's most artistically talented individual. In fact, you might say that I am artistically challenged. (No, that is not negativity. It is honesty.)

When I have an opportunity to observe a true artist applying their craft, I get very jealous of the beautiful something that can come from nothing. For example, consider the painter who takes the blank canvas and creates the artist's vision of the world around him. I am talking about the potter who, with only the slightest pressure from her hands, gives shape to the shapeless mound of clay. I am talking about how the sculptor finds beauty inside the stone.

You are your own creator. You are the artist whose vision takes the nothing in order to create the something. You are the mound of clay in your own hands.

What do you see inside yourself that provides you the inspiration to work to create greatness? Create the better you from the putty that you are. The power to create is within us all. You only need develop your artist's eye.

#143 ~ It's Worth Fighting For

In today's society, we hear a lot of talk about the concept of *partisan politics* as if it were a dirty subject. I ask you to consider how fighting for and standing up for what you believe can ever be thought to be the wrong thing to do.

Are you willing to put your beliefs on the line? Are you willing to defend the things you believe against those who would attack them as wrong?

I guess your willingness to stand for something is a reflection of the courage of your convictions. To be successful, you must be certain of who you are in the face of those who would question your reason, your ethics, and intelligence. They put you in this position just because you had the courage to disagree.

I suggest that if you cannot defend in a partisan manner what you believe, then you are simply a blind follower of the popular opinion. That is, you are a person defined by their fear to challenge head-on the overriding opinion of those around you.

Do not be afraid to challenge the ideas of others, and do not be afraid when others find the courage to challenge you back.

#144 ~ Define Yourself

You cannot be all things to all people. So who are you then? What is it in life that you value most?

What you believe, or believe in, is what defines you as a person. I am not going to suggest what you should or should not believe in. Yet there are certain traits that come out of what might be called our common shared sense of humanity. These are your core beliefs, such as integrity, love, honesty, loyalty—you get the idea.

If the right thing, as compared to the wrong thing, was so commonly understood, then we might just end up being alike. So make your mark, define yourself by careful consideration of the philosophies that shape you. Then go out and work to give shape to the world around you.

"You see, ya' can't please everyone, so ya' got to please yourself." I have found these words from the song by Ricky Nelson, "Garden Party," to pretty much be true. Just know that the success you achieve in your life depends on you being happy with the person you find yourself to be.

#145 ~ Don't Get Swept Away

Life's challenges often present themselves as a riptide along the ocean beach. The riptide, like our personal challenges, has the power to take us in a direction we do not want to go. They can suck us out and pull us under, ensuring our ultimate failure.

Rather than fighting the tide's outward pull, the actual advice to survive a riptide is to swim parallel to the shore until, at its edges, the sweeping current of the riptide diminishes enough to allow you to swim back to safety.

So go ahead, take this advice in order to find the success for which you hope. Don't just let life's challenges sweep you out to sea in a riptide of despair and frustration. We all know that from time to time, troubles will wash the sand right out from under our feet. To achieve your success, just do not lose sight of your goal. Do not waste all your energy in a fruitless effort to swim against the tide. Just be patient and let the riptide of life take you a bit out of your way. Have the courage and self-confidence to bide your time until the opportunity to again stand your ground presents itself.

Remember, do not panic! As long as you can still see the shoreline, you are not too far to swim back toward the future you desire.

#146 ~ Run Out the Clock

Is it really a possibility to preserve a victory in life by just standing pat, content just to hold on tight to all the things that you have accomplished so far?

At the end of a basketball game, with her team in the lead, the coach thinks, *All we need to do is run out the clock, and victory is ours.* That *hold on tight* philosophy rears its ugly head just prior to what is inevitably the game's dramatic change in momentum, a change that ends up stealing away her team's victory.

Though life is not a game, you similarly cannot preserve your success in any one specific moment by your decision to cease pressing forward into the next. We cannot make time stand still. It is only in a relentless commitment to keep moving forward that you can stay ahead in, or even keep up within, the game of life.

In football, coaches often implement their prevent defense at the end of the game. It is through this defensive strategy that they hope to preserve their lead and win the game. The prevent defense strategy is to sit back and protect against the other team's big play ability to beat you. Yet often, the only thing prevented through the implementation of this strategy is the team's ability to win the game.

In life, you need to keep pushing the ball up the court, as what would life be if you were only here to run out the clock? In life, you do not win by sitting back and hoping that your inaction can prevent your failure.

To win in life, you keep the pressure on by always pressing forward toward your goal.

#147 ~ Time Marches On

What does time tell us? The question is not how do we tell time, but I am asking what lesson does time teach us about how to achieve success?

Time never stops . . .
Time marches on . . .
You can't go back in time . . .

Time is always moving forward. *Tick, tick, tick.* No matter what, time marks a never-ending progress toward tomorrow. We can all take a lesson from the *always forward* attitude of time.

If you never thought twice about your direction in life or never second-guessed your decision to keep moving forward toward your goals, how could you help but succeed?

Yes, time does march on, and so can you. You can decide where you want to go and then never take a step in any direction other than toward that goal.

Listen for the tick of the clock as it marks time's ability to always keep moving forward. Then each time you hear the rhythmic ticking, you will know that you also have a choice. Choose to make every step another step in the direction of where you want to go.

#148 ~ Moonlight Feels Right

Once you have found your success, it will radiate from you like the power that radiates as light from the sun. The power of the sun warms the earth. It lights our way, and it provides the energy for the flowers to grow.

On the other hand, there is no such thing as moon glow, no such thing as moonlight. The light from the full moon is only the light from the sun reflected back to us. The moon is just an object, which, without the sun, would be dark in the sky.

The energy created by your success will shine on all those around you, just like the light from the sun illuminates the moon. When you succeed, your brilliance will allow others to shine as well.

The sun does not fear the moon, nor should you fear those who shine in the reflection of your own accomplishments. There is a beauty in the so-called moonlight reflected on the waters of the lake by our home. However, I doubt the sun is jealous or feels the need to diminish the moon's role in such an achievement.

Become the sun and you will become a beacon of success that will guide others out from their own darkness.

#149 ~ Outside Looking In

In years past, we referred to the presentation of a chance at something new as *opportunity knocking*. I do not really know, but that may have been related to the fact that, at one time in our country's history, we had many people making a living by selling products in residential neighborhoods by going door to door. At that time, when there was a knock on the door, it originally was an opportunity to buy something you had prior only wished you could one day own.

However, as the years went by, people no longer saw the knock on the door by the salesperson as representing an opportunity. People found themselves peeking out from behind the curtains in order to avoid the person at their door.

Today, we avoid unsolicited interruptions by simply screening our phone calls for the numbers we do not recognize, or worse, numbers we do recognize. Maybe you could say that opportunity no longer knocks; it rings. Yet, you will never know if you do not sometimes answer the call.

My point is not about the value of telemarketing or door-to-door sales. The point is to let you know that prejudging opportunity may just cause you to miss out. Prejudging can reduce your chances to reach the level of success you seek, and by doing so, you may one day find yourself on the outside looking in.

#150 ~ When to Say When

Surprisingly, we often find the roots of failure in a person's inability to admit to themselves that it's time to say when. It is in a person's relentless pursuit of a goal that cannot be realized where an individual can begin to first lose hope. It is this loss of hope for the long run that later robs people of their ability to achieve greatness, as that experience limits their ability to dream of something better for themselves.

You need to know when it's time to say when and when it's time to get extra creative in order to take your efforts to achieve a specific goal to the next level.

Both paths of self-determination can lead you to success and satisfaction. Just as there is satisfaction in knowing that you did what you could, it is also important to be smart enough to know when and how to move on.

Do not be afraid to take the lessons learned as your best reward for having tried.

#151 ~ The Audacity of Hope

Hope allows you to picture yourself in all that is possible. That reality was made clear by Barack Obama's choice of the title for his book *The Audacity of Hope*. How is it you could possibly ever hope to achieve the success of which you dream without possessing the internal audacity to believe the three simple words, *Yes, I can?*

I think that "hope is not just wishing, hope believes." Hope believes in the power of you as an individual. In your power to achieve whatever it is you dream. Hope is the tiny light only the dreamers can see at the end of the dark tunnel.

The energy created by President Obama's campaign slogan, *Yes we can*, is proof that hopes and dreams, no matter how audacious, really can come true.

#152 ~ Be Like the Farmer

When you make an investment in the stock market, your money must be laid on the line before a return on that investment can be claimed.

When you make an investment into a personal relationship, you must give of yourself before you can expect to have that investment returned in the form of friendship.

Individuals claim opportunities to win when they are willing to do the work before reaping their reward.

So be like the farmer and be prepared to till the soil, plant the seed, clear the weeds, and water the field before you harvest the crop that should help to define your success.

Remember, you can never harvest a positive relationship before you plant the seeds of goodwill.

#153 ~ What To Do

Merge Left—Stop Ahead—Caution . . .
First we are told *what to do!*

Then we are told *what not to do!*
No Left Turn—No Passing—No U Turns . . .

Is there really room in life for a person to be a free thinking individual with a mind of their own?

Take golf for instance. There are so many rules that the average player doesn't even know them all. Then there's the US tax code, don't even get me started about the rules the IRS has laid down in order to take our money.

Of course, the base line for success in life is that you must know and follow the rules; that is the minimum. Yet, to be really successful, you must not be afraid to make a few rules of your own.

Maybe this thought is about the uncertainty we encounter in our daily lives and our ability to overcome the fear of the uncharted. Not everyone can handle the prospect of being held responsible and accountable for their own success. Most people wouldn't want a life built solely on the rules they set for themselves.

Yet, there will be times when rules are unclear or just don't exist. In those times, when you find yourself in this spot, all alone, don't second guess your instincts. Fearlessly make a few rules of your own and get on with it. Remember, you have things you want and need to get done!

#154 ~ Take Them One at a Time

To be the winner of the road race, you only need ensure that you beat the person in front of you. I know that idea is somewhat silly in a way. In reality, you only need to have that singular goal in order to win the race. So put a target on the back of the person who is running the race in front of you. Then when the time comes where you find that you have no one else to catch, no one else in front of you, you will be the front-runner. When the path in front of you is clear, you will then be in the best position to win your race.

It is somewhat simpler if you want to be considered successful in life, as you only really need to beat yourself. Success comes when you have stretched your own limits and redefined your own possibilities. This definition of success allows you to succeed and to grow, no matter where the finish line is along your race route.

In the race of life, you do not need to finish first to be considered a winner. I am sure it is an incredible feeling to be the one who breaks the tape at the finish line in the race. Just as I am certain that it would be exciting to be the person who invented the internet, invented the lightbulb, and invented the steam engine . . . you get the idea.

Just know, in the race we run each day, as in the case of the marathon runner, all those who persevere and finish the course receive the applause.

#155 ~ Opportunity is Given

Each and every day, we are *given* opportunities to succeed. Yes, I said given! Like in someone saying, "Here it is, now what are you going to do with it?"

The opportunity to be whatever you want is yours from day one. What you choose to do with it on day one affects what opportunity or opportunities are available to you on day two. You have made your choices and have shaped your world by those choices you have made each day up until today.

You have heard it said that today is the first day of the rest of your life. Well, that is most certainly true for you and your life.

Opportunity has been yours. It has been there on a silver platter. What you do with that gift is the question. As individuals, we say that we want things, and yet we fail to even make an effort to get them. I do not mean we try, and we fail. I mean we often even fail to try. We just plain fail to take advantage of the chances we have to succeed.

I say that "opportunities in life are *given*, while your success is *earned*." Therefore, take advantage of each opportunity given, and you will eventually succeed.

#156 ~ Enjoy the View

You may never know when your journey will bring you this way again, so enjoy the view. Of course, I am talking about enjoying more than the beauty of the scenery. My point here is to *take life in*. Experience each opportunity fully as this exact opportunity will never be here again.

Every moment is remarkable, and each and every moment is unique. Yet we find ourselves—from time to time—looking around. We literally are unaware of how we got ourselves to where we are right now. It's as if we *live unconsciously*.

Each journey has many points of interest along the way . . . Notice them, stop and take them in! *Live consciously*. Not all these experiences will be momentous like your first trip to Disney or the Grand Canyon. Yet each one has the potential to become a page in your story.

You should look at your success as more than just a destination point. It is something that you can achieve through your enthusiastic enjoyment and awareness of each leg of your journey to get there.

#157 ~ Power of the Many

A single shingle cannot keep the rain from soaking through the roof of your home. It is only when many shingles are bound together with the nails of their common purpose that the single shingle can fulfill its purpose. A sole shingle cannot stand alone and hope to achieve its positive result.

This is an important lesson to understand when you are experiencing the same futility in your own individual efforts, as would a single shingle. As you pursue your objectives, you should remember to harness the *power of the many*. Never be afraid to look for what is possible when a group of people is committed to working together toward a common goal.

Together, a country put a man on the moon. Together, a country had a dream. Together, a country fought off the tyranny of a king and declared its independence.

Successful people not only realize the power that is found within the group. They are skilled in how to bring the many together and the methods of focusing the power of their common will.

Do what you can or what you must to achieve your personal objectives. Just remember to look to the power of a common purpose in order to achieve those goals you envision that are bigger than yourself.

#158 ~ The Creative Flames

Candles, though they may burn bright, burn down, and then they burn out. How will you keep your creative flames burning bright? How will you avoid the feeling of the darkness that will surround you when you no longer feel inspired?

In general, a candle does not burn out because the wick has burned down. It burns out because it has used up its fuel; as the wax burns away, so does the wick. So long as there is wax, the candle will burn bright. So long as there is oil, the lamp will burn bright.

You need to remember to fuel the fire of your own creative energy all the time. That which fuels your fire is that which inspires you to strive for the success you seek. It is within this supply of fuel that you keep your desire to succeed burning brightly.

Inspirational or motivational fuel is different for all of us. It may be, at its core, our own personal definition of what we consider defines us as successful. Is it money? Is it respect? Is it time with family and friends? The realization, that your desire for one or all these things is what ignites your inner fire, is the key to keeping that fire burning.

Knowledge of how the process works for you as an individual is most important in keeping that personal desire for success burning inside of you.

#159 ~ Make It Personal

To be successful in life, make *all* things personal. How can relationships—and make no mistake about it, relationships are the foundation of all success—not be personal?

You have probably heard it said, "I'm sorry, it's really nothing personal, it's just business." However, I believe, and I have heard it repeated by others. In sales, *people buy from people*. Now how much more personal can it get than that?

In education, your mom would state, teachers talk all day to groups of students, but that learning only takes place when the teacher makes the effort to relate to each child on a personal level.

How can you connect with anyone if you do not make it personal? To be successful by any definition in life, you must be successful in cultivating and growing successful personal relationships.

Make everything personal, and you will be successful. However, more importantly, you will be happy.

#160 ~ Dealing with Change

At 32 degrees Fahrenheit, water turns to ice.

At 211 degrees Fahrenheit, steam turns to water.

At 33 degrees Fahrenheit, ice turns to water.

At 212 degrees Fahrenheit, water turns to steam.

How flexible are you in your ability to adapt to the changing environment around you?

Some consider a person's inflexibility, which is their staunch determination to stand their ground, to be a personal strength. In the end, we must recognize that water's ability to change and adapt to the world's ever-changing stimulus is what makes it such a valuable resource.

Are you a resource on your boss's team, on your company's team, on your friend's team, and on your family's team?

Water evaporates, it flows, it is absorbed, it can become a solid, and it has the ability to fall as rain . . . To be successful, be the water!

Just go with the flow, and one day, you will have the opportunity to carve your own Grand Canyon of personal accomplishment just like the water.

#161 ~ Stressed Out

"I'm so stressed out." We have all heard people say that. Maybe we have said it once or twice ourselves. What is frustrating about that statement is that people say it as if it should be cause for us to take pity on their situation.

It is like saying, "I'm so fat!" If you are overweight, it is because you ate too much, exercised too little, or probably both. You chose the food, or you chose the couch. You also choose to feel stressed by what life brought your way and the decisions yourself made. Of course I recognize that there are medical conditions that affect an individual's ability to maintain a healthy weight, just like there are conditions which affect peoples ability to deal with stress, and that those conditions are outside of their control. I'm not talking about those types of situations.

What I am saying is that when you accept a challenge, you must understand there is likely to be stress from lots of sources. Including the stress created as your emotional insecurities conflict with your internal drive to succeed. This stress we put on ourselves occurs because we do not want to let ourselves down. It is all about not wanting to fail. This is the stress created from not wanting to let those around you down or to end up seen as a failure.

It is up to you to make the commitment to overcome. Only you can focus your energies on your plan to succeed, and only you can deal with the stresses of life within your own life.

Stress is naturally created when you care about the result of your efforts to succeed.

Stressed out . . . I say it is a cop-out. That's just life!

#162 ~ You Just Gotta' Wing It

"I didn't know if I could make the throw. Even after I threw it, I wasn't sure." This was Brett Favre in an interview after leading his first come from behind fourth-quarter victory as a Minnesota Viking in 2009. He then continued, "But sometimes you just have to wing it!"

If you want to win in life, you have to realize that not every bet is a sure thing. So sometimes, you just have to risk it all to win it all. Sometimes you just have to roll the dice to see what comes up.

You will not win them all, but you will not win any of them if you are afraid to risk it all, or if you are afraid to put it all on the line in order to win.

You cannot win if you are afraid to personally step up and just wing it. If you don't believe me, just ask Brett Favre.[1]

---

[1]   Brett Favre holds the NFL record for most interceptions. He also holds the NFL record for most touchdown passes and victories.

#163 ~ Own It

Do not go through life as a renter, moving from one philosophy to another. Make your commitment to an idea and buy in!

When you buy into a belief, it becomes you. When you buy in, you no longer need to think about each of life's many decisions. That is because your clear guiding philosophy easily defines for you and those around you who you are.

Many of us move from one fashionable set of ideas to another. The reality is that we truly never totally believe in what we say we believe in.

Put up or shut up! Place your bet and spin the wheel. If you do not put your money down, you cannot go home a winner.

When you buy into a great idea or two, you will see firsthand how your commitment to a cause will change your life.

#164 ~ Power of the Sun

When the pinecone falls from the tree, it falls with only one purpose, which is to spread the seeds that will grow tall into a new tree. With the power provided by the sun, the seed germinates starting its journey upward. Nothing can stop the process as the tree stretches toward the sun.

Which of your goals has the power of the sun to draw you upward toward your success? Do you have a goal with the power to motivate you to do whatever it takes?

Have you ever seen the tree that grows from the crack it has created in the blacktop? Nothing can stop the seed from growing into the tree it seeks to become.

Do you see any of your obstacles to be as formidable as the hard asphalt surface must seem to the seed in search of the sun?

Find your sun, and you will find a power within you so motivating that nothing can stop you from growing tall and reaching the success that you seek.

#165 ~ No Letter I in Team

There is no *I* in team, but there is in wIn!
—Michael Jordan

Michael understood that success, as a member of a team is the result of what they achieve when all work together toward a common goal. That necessity for group cohesiveness in no way allowed Michael or allows you to abdicate your personal responsibility for the role we play as individuals in achieving the victory for the team.

Individual excellence must still be the standard. That is true for all team members in pursuit of a goal. Team members must always be aware of the role that is played by each of them as *I*, an individual.

Yes, you win the game as a team but only through the team members' individual one-on-one victories throughout the contest.

The key to winning—and success—in these situations is your recognition and your acceptance of your own individual responsibility to personally excel at each given opportunity!

#166 ~ Pass the Prunes

You often will find that there is opportunity hidden within the constant challenges presented to us each day.

The challenge that stands before you today is your opportunity to snatch victory from the jaws of defeat. It is the silver lining that graces life's gray clouds. It is looking for and finding your upside in every downturn.

What we do or how we choose to react in the face of our challenges is what allows us to more than just persevere. That which actually allows us to answer the challenge is what gives us the opportunity to be slingshotted forward. As you know, you only find success through your sheer determination to keep moving forward.

Keep your eyes open for the opportunity. As you should know, the change represented by our challenges always—yes, always—accompanies opportunities to grow.

That is why when life presents you with the inevitable bowl of prunes; just know this is your chance to say good-bye to your nagging constipation. In other words, what you chose to do with the adversity is that which allows you to keep going . . . and going . . . and going. (Pun intended!)

#167 ~ Checkmate

Your actions today have consequences that have the potential to carry well into your tomorrow. These can be a positive, or these consequences can represent a negative. Either way, the choices you make or the road you choose today will have a dramatic impact on your final destination.

It is a bit like the game of chess; as in chess, you must analyze and predict how your opponent will react to each move you make. How many moves ahead should you try to anticipate? The answer is as many as you can imagine, that is, if your goal is to win the game.

A missed calculation could cost you your knight or end in a checkmate of your king. The power is in believing that even if you lose a knight, a bishop, or even a queen, you can still win. Nevertheless, you cannot afford to fail to see how a seemingly harmless move will end up exposing your king, as that wrong move will likely mark the end of the game.

Play the game of life as you play chess. Always be looking to what your next move will be and what consequences it could have in the pursuit of your goals.

#168 ~ It's the Real Thing

To be yourself, you must know yourself—by truly knowing one's self, you can then actually be your authentic self.

Knowing what you believe allows you to act consistently to support those beliefs. By acting consistently, we provide others a basis upon which they will judge our authenticity.

"Is it live, or is it Memorex?" For over thirty years, this marketing message for Memorex audio and videocassette tapes had been the very basis of their sales success. It was simple. If you wanted a more authentic recreation of an audio or video image, you had to buy Memorex tapes. Consumers' desire for the real thing played well for this company in its product sales for decades.

People also want that kind of certainty from their personal relationships as well. They do not want to be handled. They do not want to be manipulated. They just want to know that when they are dealing with you, that you are the real deal.

When others know you for who you are and what you believe, that is being authentic. It is important to remember this because when people know where you stand, they may be willing to stand with you in order to support what you clearly believe.

#169 ~ Look for the Lesson

Stop in order to take the time to ask yourself what each experience is teaching you. Take time to look for the lessons.

Understand that a lesson you endeavor to learn the first time is a lesson you never need learn again.

What is it about hitting our heads, again and again, against the brick wall of ignorance that people seem to enjoy so much?

It is like the old saying I mentioned before, "Fool me once, shame on you . . . Fool me twice, shame on me."

The lesson in these words not only supports the importance of learning from the lessons life has to offer. It goes one-step further as it clearly places the responsibility to learn from those lessons squarely on your shoulders.

Know this: your greatest knowledge will come from the lessons you take the time to realize for yourself.

#170 ~ Measure Twice

Carpenters have a rule . . . a good one, *measure twice, cut once.* If your goal is to finish the project, this rule is efficient in ensuring your success.

I have taken this rule and applied it to living a successful life. By taking the time properly to consider the options in any decision, you take a big step toward ensuring your success. So I say, "think twice, decide once."

A *think twice* philosophy can minimize impulsive mistakes and the affects of misinformation or confusion. Thinking twice ensures proper analysis of the facts and takes away the probability of making a wrong assumption.

Taking the time to make the correct decision definitely takes less effort than having to take the time to go back and do it again in order to get it right.

Imagine the level of respect you will earn when others see you as a thoughtful decision maker. A reputation for rash decisions can, and will, totally discount your opinion and your value to your team.

Whenever success is your goal, you can seldom afford not to do it right the first time.

#171 ~ The View from Above

When taking in the view from a jet plane at thirty-six thousand feet, big things seem so very small. Lakes look like puddles, farms like postage stamps, and rivers like holiday ribbon. Yet these same objects begin to regain their proper proportion as the plane begins its descent. Then at the moment of the plane's landing, all things become clear and in their proper proportion again.

The problems you face from day to day are really just the opposite in terms of perspective. Up close, personal issues generally seem larger than they really are. That thought is kind of like the idea expressed in the wording on the passenger side mirror of your car, "Objects in mirror appear closer than they are."

To put your problems into a proper perspective, you need to get away from them. Take a step back, and you will see a challenge for what it really is. Perspective is just a matter of how we see things from where we stand. In order to change your perspective and change your perception, go stand somewhere else. I promise that it will all become clearer to you from there.

#172 ~ Put Together the Puzzle

Ask by saying please . . . Say thank you . . . Share your toys . . . Yield the right of way . . . Give to those less fortunate . . . Educate yourself before forming an opinion . . . Show common courtesy . . . Respect your elders . . . Stay organized . . . Plan ahead . . . Say hello to the people you know . . . Say hello to the people you don't know . . . Acknowledge those who've helped you . . . Don't take more than your share . . . Don't take more than you need . . . Listen to your mom . . . Be patient . . . Follow through.

Do these and many other good things, and people will say that you are a good person! Yes, your success can result from any one of the many things listed above or the cumulative result of many of the things listed above. In the puzzle, each piece is small, but each piece is important. One piece is no more important than every other one if you want to see the complete picture.

Like pieces of the puzzle, each little piece of life is part of the larger picture. That means that you will never finish the picture of your success until you have placed the last of the pieces in their proper place.

#173 ~ The Choice Is Yours

The shortest distance between two points is the straight line. (One of the things I still remember from high school geometry class.) It is the quickest way from point A to point B. Given that this fact has been proven to be true, we could then call this route the fast track.

The scenic route also takes you from point A to B. It may not be the most direct route as it is not a straight line. Yet you certainly will not find the joy you will experience upon choosing this route within how it helps you to quickly reach your destination. You will find that the joy here is found to be within the journey itself.

By choosing the fast track for your life's journey, your success will be measured not just by your arrival at your destination but also by the length of time it takes you to arrive.

Should you choose the scenic path, you will find your success within the experiences you have enjoyed and grown from along the way.

The funny thing is that there is no advice here except to say . . . the choice is yours. Neither is right, neither is wrong. The choice is nothing more than one of two equally rewarding ways to skin the cat.

Only you can decide which is right for your own journey.

#174 ~ No Matter the Cost

What price must be paid in order to ensure victory?

What is the cost to you if you do not win?

The price of victory may be too high, forcing you to accept defeat before the game begins. On the other hand, the cost of losing may be so high you cannot afford to risk not winning no matter the cost.

In these two examples, the choice is not within your control. However, in these instances, the analysis of the need to act or not to act is based solely on the situation's perceived return on investment (ROI). Which means your result always will be measured against your investment of time, energy, cash, or perhaps even your integrity.

To act without this critical process of consideration is to act without the specific knowledge needed to make an informed decision. Only go all in if you believe the potential of a positive return to be greater than the probability of a negative result.

When you maximize your ROI, and you maximize the probability for success, you will then be able to find the final result you have been looking for.

#175 ~ Cookies, Peanuts, Pretzels

The flight attendant had just asked me for my preference between cookies, peanuts, or pretzels. So for a moment, I paused like most of the other passengers, not sure which to choose. As I contemplated my response, it oddly occurred to me that these options presented to me a true conundrum. No choice was superior to the other, as I like them all equally.

Then it struck me. Maybe if we want to achieve the success we desire, we should find a way to focus our energy of those things in life that *will* make a difference. We need to stop spending so much energy on making life's *nondecisions*.

Focus on those things that matter to us. By definition, they matter because the difference in outcomes will make a difference in whether or not we reach our goals.

Decide what matters most to you and focus your energy on first knowing what you want most and then on getting that thing.

By the way, I chose the peanuts. I do not really know why, but then I ask you, does it really matter?

#176 ~ Celebrate All the Victories

In football, the common philosophy is always to come away from a scoring opportunity with points. The belief is that you do not want to expend all the energy necessary to drive down the field only to come away empty-handed.

Any effort that does not take you one step closer to achieving your goals cannot be said to be a step forward. It is important that you look to ensure all your efforts successfully take you one step closer to your goals. In other words, your efforts need to score you points.

Sure, sometimes your efforts may take you a quantum leap forward, and you should certainly savor those victories. Yet just as important in your journey is the effort that produces but a single step forward.

Emerge from today having taken that single step, and then tomorrow, you will again have another opportunity to take a second, third, and fourth step forward. You will see, eventually, the cumulative nature of all your efforts will enable you to win life's big game.

Score points on every procession . . . Keep moving forward, and then you can get ready to celebrate your victory.

#177 ~ I'm Out of Ink

Have you ever noticed that the pens given away free by the bank, your insurance representative, or the local car dealership really are not very good? I mean, there just does not seem to be very much ink in them, and they go dry or fall apart before you know it.

I wonder if the businesses reason to give pens away was to let their customers know that they are special. If that is so, then answer for me the question, "What is so special about a pen that won't work next week?"

If the purpose of the pen is to advertise the name of the business who gave it to you, then I ask, "What is the value of an advertising message that ends up so quickly in the trash?"

In our quest to be successful, we all will face decisions, the result of which will reflect who we are in the eyes of those around us.

When making those critical decisions, never forget the feeling you had the moment that your free pen went dry.

What message do you want to send?

#178 ~ Set Your Bar

What I want for you in life should never be more than what you want for yourself. My aspirations can and probably will be different from your own, but they should never be greater than your own.

How then do you decide where to set the bar for your own success? Make no mistake about it, only you can set the bar. Others, your mother and me included, may do what we can to influence the bar's placement. However, only you get to decide how large a challenge you are willing to accept.

You can consider opinions, and you can research facts. Yet in the end, only you will write the definition of your own success. It is your responsibility to place your own bar if you are to enjoy the satisfaction in reaching your goals.

Failure to place the bar may mean you avoid any chance of disappointment, but it also means you have eliminated any chance to claim satisfaction from the achievement of success as the realization of a goal.

Without clearly defined goals and objectives, you cannot feel the satisfaction of having achieved your successful result. You may be able to feel happy about how things turn out. My point, however, is you cannot take credit for the job well done as there is no real satisfaction if you accidentally become successful.

#179 - Ask for Help

One day you will be my age, and you will not be able to read the words on these pages without a pair of reading glasses. Cheaters, they call them cheaters. Why cheaters? Should I feel like a bad person because I can no longer read the fine print without a bit of help?

People my age joke about their cheaters. In groups, we laugh nervously as we share our common affliction. I think we actually all feel a bit inadequate and even a bit embarrassed by this seemingly inevitable sign of growing old.

I guess that reality begs the question as to why we should feel inadequate or embarrassed when we are forced to put on our cheaters.

You will find the lesson regarding your journey to be successful in the fact that few people achieve success all on their own—with no outside help, that is.

Do not be embarrassed to ask for some help in achieving your goals. Reading glasses are not cheating, and asking for help is nothing for you to be embarrassed about.

One day you will not be able to read these words, as they will be but a blur. But it will be okay, just go ahead and just put on your cheaters. I am sure that no one will be looking!

#180 ~ Constructive Criticism

Be gracious when receiving criticism. Accept the opinions of others in their constructive attempt to help you become a better you. Know that you cannot always know better—just as you certainly cannot ever know it all.

It is most definitely a good thing to have unshakable confidence. That, however, does not mean turning a deaf ear to the shared opinions offered respectfully by others. It is the helping hand that is given within these opinions that you can use to help you reach your goals.

But then again, just because the opinions of others collectively fly directly in the face of what you believe, does not make what you believe wrong. Just like the act of stamping down your foot when trying extra hard to make a point does not make you right. Just in the same way that pounding your fist in a tantrum will not help you get what you want.

Be open to new ways of looking at things and accepting of the perception of others in the way they see us. It just may help you to see the real potential for a better you.

#181 ~ Take Notice

Success loves company. That is why you should start by acknowledging the accomplishments of those around you. It sends an important message when you take the opportunity to recognize other people's efforts and their role in your success or their own success.

Exciting things are happening around you every day. Watch closely, and you will see people who are making the extra effort, people committed to going the extra mile, and people who will stop at nothing as they pull out all the stops in order to accomplish their goals.

These people should be your heroes. These people should be your role models. You should acknowledge these people, as they are the very same people who have helped you imagine what is possible in all fields of endeavor.

These efforts do not have to be equal to putting a man on the moon in order to deserve a pat on the back. When you take the time to give a little credit where the credit is due, you will be surprised by positive energy created that will benefit everyone involved.

While at the same time, it is equally important that you respect yourself enough to acknowledge your own personal growth. I do not suggest this kind of self-admiration in order to give yourself a big ego, just take the time to give yourself a lift toward reaching your goals by giving you own self a small pat on the back from time to time.

#182 ~ Respect the Date

If a special event is important enough to remember, it is important enough to remember correctly.

A birthday card that arrives in the mail precisely on a friend's birthday is simply more special than the card that comes a few days later. Having your card arrive on time says something more powerful about you as a person and about your relationship as friends than any Hallmark writer ever could.

The same card received two days later just does not say the same thing as if it had been on time. *Belated* birthday wishes may as well read *deflated* birthday wishes.

Respect your relationships by respecting those special dates within each other's lives enough to remember them correctly.

You know that success in life is often built on the little things. On the outside, this may seem to be one of the smallest. However, showing you care for others by caring enough to recognize the special events in their lives will certainly make you a bigger person in their eyes.

If that is not one way to spell success, I do not know what is.

#183 ~ Find the Common Thread

Look for the common thread that will connect seemingly disconnected and distant things. The power to achieve your success is likely to be found within the power of your ability to realize those connecting relationships.

This interconnectivity of all that is around us is proven by the simple fact that at the same moment I sit in my living room looking out at the frozen lake in front of my house here in Wisconsin, I am connected to you as you sit in your living room looking out at the Pacific Ocean in California.

As far apart as those two worlds may seem, we are connected. There is a connection because the water from my lake runs into the Wisconsin River. The Wisconsin River then mixes with the waters of the mighty Mississippi that then flows into the Gulf of Mexico. The gulf then connects with the Atlantic Ocean. Of course, the Atlantic Ocean touches up against that very same Pacific Ocean you see right outside your window.

Know that all things share a connection. Respect the connections, promote the connections, and utilize the connections to achieve your objectives.

Remember that this connectivity means that your accomplishments connect to the ability of many other people to reach objectives of their own. This idea means that we really are all in this together. Thus, those things that connect us also have the power to help us all succeed as well.

#184 ~ Deal With It

We are not all great at everything we do. It is not possible to be, as they say, a true jack-of-all-trades. Some tasks are bound to make you feel uncomfortable. That is, some things are bound to be outside your comfort zone.

Well then, you have a few choices. You can accept these limitations, or you can define your limitation as a weakness and work to overcome it. Maybe your discomfort when faced with this sort of challenge is nature's way of letting you know what your weaknesses really are.

We become uncomfortable when we take on that which we have little skill successfully to accomplish. The power of this built-in personal alarm system is found only when we listen to its signals. It is through that act of listening that we are able to know what we need to do in order to improve.

When you let a weakness limit your potential, you are succumbing to your fear. When you focus your energy to turn your weakness into strength, you find yourself with unlimited potential.

So be honest with yourself about those things that leave you feeling uneasy, and you will be halfway home in your effort to turn each of your weaknesses into strengths.

#185 ~ Great Minds

Everything you ever needed to know about how to become a success in life, someone else already knows. Yet there we are, each day needlessly hitting our heads against the same wall, needlessly chasing our own tails. The result, we end up learning that the wall is hard, and our tail is attached. There we all are unnecessarily rediscovering the spoke so we can each reinvent the wheel. Why?

The force for success is strong within all of us, just as the *Force* was strong within *Star Wars* character Luke Skywalker. But for him to be successful—as defined by becoming a Jedi Knight—he had to look to Master Yoda.

You also should look to find your own Master Yoda, your own mentor. Just as Yoda revealed to Luke the power of the *Force*, so too will your mentor reveal to you the opportunities for success that surround you. He/she will also be there to warn you about the dangers of the *Dark Side*.

You do not need to learn all lessons for yourself in order to see the value of what experience has to teach. That is why I have written these books for you. Great minds think alike. Find yourself another great mind that is willing to share what he/she thinks with you.

#186 ~ Look Before You Leap

We all have many things, many people, and many organizations in which we believe in the justness of their cause. Yet, there is a fundamental difference between belief in what you know and faith in what is unknown. That, I suppose, is why they refer to going out on a limb as a *leap of faith*.

I cannot say, nor do I suppose to suggest, that I have the right to tell you spiritually what to believe in. However, I do want to suggest that you find real faith, and I hope you are lucky enough to believe in something bigger than you are. Faith in a higher power has been the cause of many wars and many more miracles. Without a personal faith in God, some would say that you are less than whole.

I am not saying that I am right. I am only saying that in order for you to find your true happiness, you must have the courage to believe in those things that you cannot see or prove. With the power of your faith to fall back on, you will find that you then have the courage to stand up in the face of those who doubt you. You then will more easily access within yourself the power to succeed.

You have to wonder, in the end, was it you who found the courage to succeed, or did something bigger than all of us instill it in you?

#187 ~ Coming Full Circle

This concept of having come *full circle* is a combination of words that presents itself to us as being the culmination of a wonderfully successful journey.

I wonder what those people think to be so amazing? As the idea of coming full circle only means that you are back where you began. I hope, no, I expect that your goals are a bit loftier than to live a life only to end up back where you started.

Yes, the circle is safe. By following the circular path, you will never make a bad decision. Your way will always be well marked to ensure you do not get lost. Why, the idea of having come full circle even has a warm and fuzzy feeling about it.

The completion of the circle represents both the end and beginning. Yet the thought of your life as a circle should make you dizzy. It does me! Then I never really did like the teacups at Disney World. In fact, just the thought of looking at life as nothing more than a never-ending circle makes my stomach a bit queasy.

I just hope that the day you announce that you have arrived, it is somewhere different from where you began.

#188 ~ Santas Are Down

One day each year, sometime after Christmas, your mom always takes down the santas and puts up the snowmen. One day, it's santas, and the next day, it's snowmen. Did you notice? Did you let her know how wonderful it looked and how much you appreciated the effort? You probably did, but me, I am a man, and sometimes these kinds of things can slip by unnoticed and unmentioned.

In life, you find that every day the people around you are working hard to stand out and reach a level of personal excellence that meets their own goals. Do you notice their efforts? Do others notice when you make an extra effort to get the little things right?

Successful people key themselves into the little things. That is because they know it is the little things that make the biggest difference. Successful people know how much effort they put into achieving their own success, and they mark their efforts by all the little things they do.

To achieve your success, you should focus on the little things. To be a good person, you should recognize the little things. Keep your eye out for the little things as they really can make the biggest difference of all.

#189 ~ It's in the Box

Where did the idea come from that in order to be successful you had to, as they say, think *outside of the box*? If we were only able to find success outside the box, then I submit to you that no one would have ever invested himself or herself in the construction of that box in the first place.

Perhaps we should all see the box simply as a metaphor for the conventional wisdom of what is necessary to achieve success. Perhaps you should consider that you could not achieve true success by solely thinking outside the box. Rather, you will more likely find what you are looking for by consistently striving for excellence within it.

In the world of football, each team, through diligent study, knows precisely what their opponent will be likely to do in any given situation. Nevertheless, the team that invariably wins the game is the one that executes most consistently.

Of course, there are examples of the occasional outside the box trick play that miraculously wins the game. However, I am still committed to the belief that it was only the team's successful execution of the expected that allowed their outside the box play to work.

So run a trick play or two in life, if you must. Just never forget that the game of life is won by those who consistently execute effectively within that box of conventional wisdom.

#190 ~ Nothing Better to Say

I have always hated when people in positions of authority felt they needed to use the words, *because I said so*. As a kid, you would often hear those words from your mother and father. Especially during those times you dared to question our authority. I might actually believe that I had opportunity to hear these words used more than most while I was growing up from my parents.

As I have grown older, I often find myself wondering why people in authority have such a profound lack of ability to explain themselves. How it is that those who see themselves as so infallible simply cannot justify their positions logically. Rather, they must flex their authoritative muscles in their effort to get things done their way.

What I have come to understand is that these words, *because I said so*, are nothing more than a last grab for control by those who find themselves powerless to rationally defend their positions. I know that seems a bit harsh. Yet saying such is no harsher in degree than the underlying stupidity of the words themselves. (And yes, I have said them.)

As a successful individual, you should strike these words from your vocabulary and stand by your convictions with a clearly articulated purpose. When you make the effort to help those around you to clearly understand, you will find that they probably will not feel the need to question you in the first place.

#191 ~ Loyalty

You are where you are today because others helped you get there. People lent you a hand, offered advice, and took time to teach you how. Most of them offered their help with no expectation of return on their investment in you. It was a gift from their heart. Maybe you never even asked for the help, yet they gave. They were just there willing to lend you a hand.

So what do you owe those who have helped you to where you are today? Successful people pay back that kind of generosity with loyalty and friendship.

Many people have helped you to reach your level of success. Each step was only that, a step that moved you upward. With all the help you have received, you may find that your personal growth over time may cause you to outgrow certain relationships.

Let me ask you again, what is the price you are willing to pay for your success? Not all things can stay as they were, but the advice here is not to take those who have given you the leg up for granted. Do not turn your back on those who were willing to lend you the shirt off their own back in order to help you succeed.

When you remember to, as my mom's father always said, "Dance with thems that brung ya," your loyalty will become the basis of your success. As such, it will also prove to provide you its own long-term reward—your happiness.

#192 ~ Make Time to Pee

Whoever said time flies when you are having fun probably never needed to bring a project in on time and under budget. You see, nothing makes time fly by faster than having personal responsibility for completion of a clearly defined task with a deadline.

Focused on success, we often throw ourselves headlong into these projects, thus losing our perspective of time. However, the most dangerous thing about this level of effort and commitment is that it can cause us to forget all about our most basic responsibility. That is, our responsibility to take care of ourselves.

We are talking about the simple stuff like setting aside a few minutes to sit and eat lunch, read a book, meet with friends, or spend time with your family. We are talking about taking time for all the little things in life that you cannot afford to overlook.

Of course, successful people go the extra mile doing whatever it takes. However, successful people do not define themselves by who they are at work. Set your goals for your success at work as well as separately within your personal life. Just make sure you leave a few minutes in your schedule each day to pee.

#193 ~ Along for the Ride

"Are we there yet?" These are the four words that, when driving, my dad dreaded to hear coming from the backseat. When we were kids, my dad saw such inquiries as his kids just being very impatient. I would like to suggest that as kids, we were just very *goal oriented.*

You almost never hear adults willing to pose such a question. Adults are too mature and too polite. If you watch carefully, you will see that most adults are seemingly content to just sit back and go along for the ride.

As annoying as it may sound to you, I suggest that in your journey through life, you never lose touch with the little kid who was always willing to ask, "Are we there yet?" It is that urgent energy and youthful anticipation that will help you stay focused on moving forward toward your goals.

Though I suggest you never stop asking the question, I also suggest that you maybe refrain from asking it aloud. This is especially true when you are sitting in the backseat of your grandfather's car.

Go ahead, get out of life's backseat and never be content merely to go along for the ride. Be the driver! When you are the driver, it is always okay to challenge your own progress on the road to your own success.

#194 ~ Define Your Best

"But I did my best . . ." So when is this statement a reason for celebration, and when is it nothing more than an excuse?

If your effort to achieve your goal requires you to give 100 percent of all that you have, and through that *best* effort, you succeed, then doing your best is certainly a reason to celebrate. Know this, if your goals are realistic, that is, they are attainable, then your best can only result in one thing, and that is your *success*.

If the goals that you set are realistic and yet the result is not the desired result, then your claim that you gave it your best effort is nothing more than an excuse.

You have the talent, you have the skill, and you have the determination. When you focus these attributes and you work hard, you will succeed. Your best will end up being more thsan good enough.

Do not lean on the words *I did my best* as an excuse for not reaching your goals. Maybe for today you set the bar a bit too high, and your best was not enough to get you there. Just know it is not the goal's fault. Know that tomorrow you will be better, and the day after that, you will be better yet. Given time and your commitment to continue to grow, the achievement of the goal you have set will get closer every day. The best, your best is yet to come, and that leaves you all the possibilities of what you can achieve tomorrow.

#195 ~ Find Your Inner Peace

You will often find that the success you experience throughout your life is found within the harmony you have created between you and the world around you. Some may see this as the ability of an individual to make silk out of a sow's ear. It is all about making the most in life from what you are given.

It is your adaptability to adjust to the environment in which you must work that provides predictability of your success as the result. If you are not happy, you have three clear choices: complain, quit, or search to find harmony. Finding harmony is nothing more than finding ways to fit your round peg into whatever square hole is presented to you.

Many would-be successful people bring themselves down by their constant need to focus on the negative. They skip off track by the wrongful allocation of their misdirected energies.

However, those who win are those who persevere in their search to find harmony within their lives and flourish by their everyday choices to celebrate the positive.

#196 ~ Old Man River

The banks of the river do not impede its progress as it flows toward the sea. The banks of the river do not impinge its power or limit its beauty. As individuals, we flow within our own banks of social norms and personal ethics.

Though these banks clearly define our direction, they do not limit our potential to progress. In fact, the presence of a river's banks can actually speed its flow, for what is a river without banks but potentially a swamp.

As a river's narrowing banks squeeze the flow, its water gains speed, gains ability to generate power, and arguably, the rush of waters could be said to make it all more beautifully breathtaking.

To achieve the success you desire, do not fight against the banks but look to those parameters to provide an additional rush of forward motion.

When the river pushes outside its banks, it could be said to have lost focus and lost purpose as it creates a flood of stagnant backwaters.

Know that it is the limits within our lives, as defined by the banks of the river, which allow us successfully to run toward our own goals.

#197 ~ Run with the Wild Horses[2]

The wild horses of the great Western plains run free without fear, without artificial fences, and without self-imposed limits. When, in the living of your life, you run free—throwing caution to the wind like those wild horses—you empower yourself to set aside your fears. When you break free from your self-imposed limits, what you will find is the freedom to face your fears and not feel scared.

You see, it is the fear of taking the next step toward our goals that has corralled more dreams than any obstacles we must overcome to achieve them.

When you throw caution to the wind, it is not that the unknown is any less frightening. It is not that achieving your goals will be any less challenging. However, by doing so, you give yourself the freedom to run with the wild horses; you free yourself to achieve all that you can dream.

Run with the wild horses toward your dreams, and you will never look back with regret to ask yourself, "Is this what my life has become?"

---

[2] Based on song lyrics by Natasha Bedingfield

#198 ~ Off to See the Wizard

In the movie *The Wizard of Oz*, the wizard pushed all the buttons as he sat in front of all the controls. With a flip of a switch, his voice boomed out, "I am the great and powerful Oz," or so he said. In the end, we find that despite all the bluster and despite all the show, the wizard was just a man.

Sometimes we find ourselves falling into the trap of believing that we are the all-powerful wizard. We want to be the one pushing the buttons and pulling all the levers. As the wizard, we want to control all the things around us. We end up caught in the *wizard trap*. That is our need to tell friends, coworkers, and family members how great we are . . . how lucky they are . . . how everything will work out all right if they listen and do it our way.

In the movie, we finally realize the wizard's real power was in his ability to help others to lift themselves up. The lion had courage the entire time. The tin man had a heart the entire time. The scarecrow had a brain the entire time. All they needed was someone to believe in them and who could help them to believe in themselves.

To become a true success, become the wizard. I am not talking about the almighty and all-powerful one who sits behind the big curtain. Just be the person who takes great joy in helping to lift up those around you in order to help them to reach their full potential.

#199 ~ Easy Way Out

So who was it that demonized the idea of taking *the easy way out* in the first place? Does it sound smart to you if I were to say, "I think I'll take the most difficult path possible in order to reach the success I seek?"

My goodness, if there were an easy way to reach your goals and a much more difficult path that brings you to the same end, then for crying out loud, why would you punish yourself by not taking the most direct route?

Oh my! I can hear the cries of those whiners now, bemoaning the rewards of overcoming the obstacles and the self-worth gained from the struggle. (I've also been heard to promote the value of the struggle.) Sure, any goal worth its salt is worth committing to the struggle to achieve it. But that's not my point.

"The easy way . . . the words just roll off the tongue. It all just makes sense—why would you not want to take the *path of least resistance?*

Stop allowing others to make life more difficult than it need be and take the easiest way you can possibly imagine on the road to your success. Then, when you get there first, just sit back and relax while you wait for the arrival of all the others!

#200 ~ Hammer It Home

The carpenter carefully positions the nail before he strikes with his hammer. Like anyone trying to teach a lesson, share an idea, or make a point, the carpenter's nail must be struck many times in order to fully drive the point home.

It is like what you have pointed out to me repeatedly. That is, you are now able to tell when I have a specific point I want to make in these books. All because I hit on that recurring theme over and over again.

Successful people know that if they want to have an impact on the opinions of those around them, they need to repeatedly reformulate and restate their argument until they make their point. Advertisers know that if they want to make their message heard, they must repeat it relentlessly.

The carpenter does not expect to drive in the nail with a single blow of the hammer. Why should you then believe any differently about your ideas? In order for you successfully to change minds, you must commit to pounding home your point.

#201 ~ Can't Stop the Rain

Worry about those things you can control or which you can exert influence. I think that people expend too much energy worrying about the things in life that are outside of their control. Things like the weather—why would you worry about what the weather will be like? Can that mental effort and expended energy change the result? No, you cannot stop the rain!

Say you have an outdoor event organized for the weekend. My advice is not to spend your time worrying about the weather, but to make use of your time to plan. If you are focused on worrying about the forecast, that will not stop the rain. When you focus your energy on what you can control, your plan for the *what if*, you help to ensure a successful event even if it does rain.

Many things in life are within your control . . . Work to control them! In many instances, what you do will have an influence on how things turn out. You should work to influence those! Unfortunately, most things are outside of your control or influence. I suggest that you plan for those!

When the weatherman calls for rain, have no worries . . . Just plan to bring your umbrella!

#202 ~ Have Courage

A leader is more than someone who stands at the front of the line. A leader is an individual who not only has a personal vision of what is necessary for the group to meet its goals, they also are a person who can clearly paint that picture so that the people around him or her can all aspire to achieve the same results.

Success as a leader starts with the courage of an individual to say what he/she believe to be true. Courage is also the willingness of that person to stand up for that belief. Do you have that kind of courage? Are you willing to put what you believe on the line for the good of others?

A true leader is willing to risk those kind of slings and arrows to achieve greater good for themselves and for those whom they lead.

I have seen where the person, who they say is in charge, simply has been selected by management to be in charge. However, I personally believe that true leaders emerge from the group. A true leader is lifted up from within the ranks of the group, pushed forward by its members to accept the responsibility of the leader's role. The group bases their choice on the power of their new leader's ideas and ideals. Only with the power drawn from the group, can a leader muster the courage and control necessary to lead the group to achieve their goals.

#203 ~ Search for Perfection

"Get over yourself!" As a firstborn child myself, I have heard it said that many psychological experts seem to believe that firstborn children can be obsessed with perfection. Well, having firsthand experience in this area, I might have to admit that they just might be right. However, it is not just the firstborn. We can all can be caught up in our own personal search for perfection—sometimes to the very detriment of all else.

I am not talking about or suggesting acceptance of *good enough* as the answer. Perhaps a small dose of reality can help us to put our relentless pursuit of perfection in perspective.

Nothing is perfect . . . nor do we have the ability to create or claim perfection. So then, where does this driving dissatisfaction with our best effort come from? What drives us to chase what is not possible? I do not know the answer to those questions. However, what I do know is that you will more likely find the happiness you seek within the acceptance of yourself and the things around you as they are.

If you pause to take it all in, you will see the world around you as more than just good enough. You will see that the world around you is nearly perfect when you are able to accept it for what it is, and accept yourself for who you are.

#204 ~ Stand in Their Shoes

For me, selling is not getting the customers to accept my perspective; it is showing them that what I sell meets their needs from their own perspective.

My success in selling over a lifetime is nothing more than my ability to relate successfully to people—though I must admit not all people. Of course, as everyone knows, you cannot win them all. Nevertheless, my ability to relate has always come from a strong belief in my need to stand in the other person's shoes. That is a strong belief that tells me that if I am to help them, there is a definite need for me to see the world from their point of view.

You will find success in all aspects of life within your own heightened awareness of the fit of someone else's shoes, and I know how much you love shoes. Now, what is it you are waiting for? Get out there then, and try on a few pair. Then you will see how many more people you can help.

#205 ~ Keep Your Eyes Open

You have asked me many times, "Dad, where do all these thoughts you've written down here come from?" My answer is always the same—life. I try to live each day with my eyes wide open to what is going on around me. There are lessons you are shown each and every day. The question you have to ask yourself is, *Are your eyes open wide enough to see them for what they are?* That is, as the key to your future success?

In our world, we base everything on cause and effect. It is an awareness of the successful person to the goings-on around them that allow them to take away the lessons from their experiences. If I do this, what will happen? If I do that, how will my outcome possibly change?

If you cannot see clearly, I suggest that you get your eyes checked. That is because you do not want to miss what life has to teach you.

Keep your eyes open to the possibility that you can repeat any successes. That is, if you have made the effort to see clearly how that success was achieved the first time around.

#206 ~ Find Your True North

In any journey, a person can get lost along the way. That is why sailors have long charted their course against the North Star—what they called their *true north*.

On your journey, you have started to reach some of the goals for which you have set for yourself. However, that does not negate the need for you to have a point of reference to help you to stay the course.

What your true north should be, I cannot tell you. However, having a core belief system, a moral compass, by which you chart your course only increases the chance that you will one day arrive and enjoy your own view from the top.

You may have found your true north written within the pages of these books I have created for you. If that is so, then I will have more than done my job. However, if what I end up accomplishing is no more than to create in you a desire to define your own beliefs, I will also have done my job.

Look out into the dark night sky that represents your unwritten future. Trust me when I say that what you believe about success, and what you have learned so far about how to get it, will be more than enough safely to guide you to wherever it is you want to go!

#207 ~ You Gotta' Believe

Nothing drives and motivates a winner more than someone telling him or her that "it can't be done!" So what will you do when faced with this level of doubt? You must remember that only you can set the limits regarding what you are able to achieve, and mostly, those limits exist only in your mind.

You see, your checking account does not have a limit on what your company can deposit. Your family does not have a limit to how much you can love them, and your favorite charity does not have a limit to how much time you can give.

When you deny others the opportunity to define for you who you are and what you can achieve, you give yourself the opportunity to define the possibilities for you to go all the way and become a winner.

When you fight back the efforts of others to put you in a box of limited potential, you give yourself permission to be a winner. Then, when you believe in yourself, you are a winner!

#208 ~ Offer a Hand Up

Let me remind you of the responsibilities with which I have entrusted you. Firstly, you are to do more than just read. You are to apply what you have learned from the books that I have written for you. Second and more importantly, it is your responsibility to share with others what you have learned as well.

It is never the wrong time for you to share your ideas. When you do, you can help someone else find his or her success. It is never too late to give of yourself to help others.

By offering a philosophical helping hand up, you will have the opportunity to see firsthand the power your ideas have to lift others to higher levels than they thought possible.

From time to time, you may find one of your ideas to have been wrong. Well, get used to it; it happens. At least when you are sharing that experience with another, you can help each other to learn a new and more powerful lesson from that experience.

Life at the top can be lonely if you do not make a commitment to help others achieve the same kind of success. Do not be afraid to invite a few friends to come along with you on your journey. There is plenty of room at the *top* for everyone.

#209 ~ Practice Makes Perfect

The idea that practice makes perfect is not one subscribed to by the parent of a tone-deaf musician. That is clearly an example where the search for perfection is stymied by a clear lack of certain basic abilities. Yet in most situations, perfection is elusive solely because the individual practices imperfectly. In other words, they practiced the wrong technique or the technique wrong.

As business legend Harvey MacKay suggested, "It is only perfect practice that makes perfect!"

As you work toward your goals, you must first be brutally honest with yourself; do you have the necessary skills? Secondly, you must ensure that, as you work to perfect your golf swing or any other talent, you are practicing technically sound techniques.

If you are honest and do have the necessary skills, then you can head for the homestretch by finding a qualified coach or mentor, a person who you can look to for solid direction and instruction.

Do not forget, that without the ability for perfect practice, perfection and your success will always remain elusive and just out of reach.

#210 ~ Graduation

Successful people always do the right thing!
—Kristine Pokrandt
September 17, 2009

Sometimes it is hard to know what the right thing is. The lines between opposites such as right and wrong can, from time to time blur as circumstances affect perceptions. Maybe some things are simple, black and white, if you will. However, doing what is right is not as easy as it sounds. Are we talking about what is right for you? Do we consider the fact that what is right for some may not be right for all?

One of the most important of all the traits and beliefs that your mom and I tried to instill in our children was a somewhat clear perspective of what the right thing is in any given situation. Yet the day you called home and shared this one-sentence revelation was one of the proudest days of my life.

How can doing the right thing ever be wrong? The answer, it can't! How can a person possibly be sure that their decision is going to turn out to be the right one? That is, right for them and right for all those around them. The answer to that question is, they can't. The fact is that some people become so afraid of not doing the right thing they end up doing the wrong thing by failing to make any decision at all. They sit, frozen by their fear.

Why is knowing right from wrong so difficult? I say step in out of the cold and set your fears aside. Although you can never abdicate your responsibility to do what is right and what you believe to be best. The expectation is that you can only do your best in your effort to do what is right.

With all the lessons recorded within the pages of these three books, know that you have actually had the final word. You could call the above quote about successful people taken from a conversation we had months back, your passing grade on your final exam. In this moment and for years to come, you will be your own judge. You will decide for yourself what you believe to be right for all concerned.

In the end, you will record your own thoughts on the subject of how to achieve your own success. You will define for yourself what it is your experience teaches you. I know from the conversations we have shared, like the one that brought forth your idea about right and wrong, that you have assembled all the tools necessary to achieve that success you so richly deserve. Now go out and do what is right!

King of the Hill

*How to Stay a Success Once
You Become One*

by Kristine's dad

Dear Kristine,

This is the start of your fourth book. However, I haven't yet given you your third book as it is still being edited by your mom. Nevertheless, I just finished reading the book *Arguing With Idiots* by Glenn Beck and some of his words inspired me to share his ideas. In his chapter on economics, he quotes a study by the Congressional Budget Office that says that the richer a person is, the smaller percentage of income gain they will experience the following year. In fact, the US Treasury Department found that the richest .01 percent of Americans at the time of the study, experienced the largest *declines* of income over the following ten years. That is probably no surprise, as they had nowhere to go but down. However, the surprise is that the decline in their income was a whopping 65 percent. This means that the king of the hill today will be back climbing, scratching, and struggling like everyone else tomorrow. Imagine, the study showed that only 25 percent of those on top today will still be on top ten years from now.

So what does that have to do with you, my dear? In thought #12 of your first book, I shared with you my philosophy that what was good enough to get you to where you are today will not be enough to keep you there. I love being right, and now I have statistical proof as to the fact. (Thanks, Glenn.)

It is like the theory I've come across called *regression to the mean.* Basically, the theory says that if you find that today is great . . . hang on because the odds are that tomorrow will not be as good. What that means is that average is average. If you flip a coin, the odds are one out of two that it will come up heads, and one out of two that it comes up tails. Yet if you have already flipped for five heads in a row, the overall odds grow better that the next flip will come up heads. Regression to the mean theory predicts that eventually you will come back to the fifty-fifty probability you started with. Even though the odds on each single flip of the coin are still just one chance in two, the deck seems to stack against a continuation of any current trend.

I have to wonder what was different about those 25 percent of top-income earners who were able to maintain their income in the top .01 percent? Regression to the mean theory flows backward in the direction of what is average. So those .01 percent had to swim against the tide. What did those people do in order to beat the odds? What did they do to fight the current? Well, if I knew the answer to those questions, then you would likely one day inherit one heck of a lot of money. That is because having that knowledge would be worth more than a king's ransom.

So is it luck? *Yes.* Is it planning? *Yes.* Is it knowledge? *Yes.* Is it hard work? *Yes.* The point I am making here is that it is one thing, or it is many things. Call it the X factor or factors that allowed each of those individuals to remain king of their hill. Maybe they believed in and lived by some of the philosophies that I am going to share with you in this book. They probably do, along with some other really important lessons their unique life experience has taught them.

You could blame the backsliding tendency that returns us all to average on gravity. For example, the mountain they each aspired to climb only goes downward in all directions once they reached its geographical peak, which the *.01 Percent Club* represents. That simple fact alone should make one wary of resting on one's laurels once you have finally experienced the view from the top. Specifically, one wrong step, and back you go in the direction from which you just came. You need to resolve yourself to the fact that you can never let your guard down. You can never stop learning, growing, or striving. If you do, your one step forward will quickly become two-three-or four quick steps back.

So what Glenn's book reminded me, which also stands as a lesson for you, was to be ever vigilant as the current always flows against our progress. We need to remember to keep pressing forward into the headwind that blows back at us as regression to the mean theory.

In the same Treasury Department study, cited by Glenn above, data showed that the bottom 20 percent of income earners from 1996 to 2006 saw incomes grow at a rate of 233 percent. I guess that is why they say, "You can't hold a good man down." (No sexism intended.) When at the bottom, there is only one way to go, and that is up. When at the top, there is only one way to go, and that is down. The idea is both exciting and scary at the same time. However, more importantly, the challenge of the opportunity to win should motivate us all.

So why have I written you another book now, you might ask? Well, it is certainly not because you are queen of any of those California hills. However, you did start at the bottom, and you have made progress. It is like the Boy Scout motto that says, *Be prepared!* So I want you to be prepared as one day, you will find yourself enjoying your own view from the top. Maybe your *top* will not be in the top .01 percent of income earners. But no matter, whatever vantage point will one day define for you your ultimate success, that vantage point will surely provide you a high level of personal satisfaction in realizing you have arrived. To keep that feeling, first make note of what it took to get there, then focus on what it will take to remain atop that hill. That is why I am sharing these thoughts with you now, ahead of what I believe to be the eventuality of your arrival at the *top*. It is all about helping you to be prepared for when that time comes.

So here we are again. I have written you another collection of thoughts on the subject of success; again in hopes that I can give you guidance on how to achieve it. However, I now also hope that I can provide you ideas as to what you must do in order to maintain it.

Maybe my collection of these observations has now become an obsession or, as your mom might say, a really bad habit. Sometimes, due to this bad habit, I cannot get to sleep at night. I lay restless with an idea rattling around so loudly that I just have to climb out of bed and write it down. Then there are early mornings where something in a dream may trigger a glimmer of an idea that I must record before I can even consider going back to sleep. There are times when I am talking with you or someone else, and within the conversation is the seed of an idea that I just have to write down. Then there are the times where I may be reading a book, like Beck's *Arguing with Idiots*, and a point that the author makes sends my mind in another direction. When these ideas pop up, I just have to stop in order to write my reflections down.

A couple weeks ago, I suggested that you start to write down your own observations about the world around you. I said this because the observation you had just shared seemed to me to be so darn powerful and profound. Your reply, "My words are your words." I have to be honest, that response almost made me cry. However, the reality is that every artist paints from the same palette of colors, and every masterpiece is painted using the same tools. I may have helped you mix a few colors, but you clearly see the world through your own colored glasses. The manufacturer of the canvas is not the artist any more than the company who made the brushes can claim credit for the beautiful expression of the artist's inspiration. From the beginning, I had only hoped to provide you with tools, mental tools, by which you would be able to navigate through life's maze and come out on the other side a more successful person. What you have done with my tools has nothing more to do with me than the easel can claim credit for the masterpiece.

I say, you may want to argue as to whether you are the artistic creator of your own success. However, you need to know that this book "King of the Hill: How to Stay a Success Once You Become One" is just another palette of colors that are now at the tip of your artist's brush. Within the colors of the palette lies the potential for you to create a masterpiece. Nevertheless, the colors of the paint on the palette provide you no promise of that level of excellence. It is all up to the artist, and make no mistake about it—you are a talented artist.

As you know, only you can define the route your climb will take. Only you decide when you have reached your goals. Maybe you can look at these books, given as gifts to you, as steps on the ladder. My original "Success," followed by "Next Level," and then "View from the Top" have proven more powerful in your life than I ever would have hoped. I know that these ideas have allowed you to lift up yourself. So take "King of the Hill" and use it in order to facilitate your continuing trip upward.

Even as I type this, I find myself smiling at the thought of your statement that, "My words are your words." Know this, my words are just words shared with me by others whom I have respected. To your advantage, you can now find all these ideas in four easy-to-read sources. That is why I tell you to write down your observations. If you learn half as much about yourself through this process of defining what it is you believe, as I have about my own self, it will be the best investment in the determination of who you are that you could ever make.

Get ready as you approach the necessity to defend your position as king of your own hill. Staying at the top will take every bit as much energy as you will have expended in your journey to get there. My challenge to you is to beat the odds and hold your ground.

Take this tool I've given you and use it to beat back the doubters, the cheaters, and the competitors who will look to bring you down. I will say, but only for the purpose of consistency, that you should take these thoughts to heart, not necessarily as the truth but as food for thought and consideration. Read and reread what I have written, and you'll see an ever-changing palette of lessons emerge from these pages.

In the end, only you will write your own story. I can only hope that I see a few of my own words among the pages you write once you declare you have arrived.

Love always,

Dad

Contents: King of the Hill

#211 ~ Great Minds Think Alike

In order to maximize your own potential, you should surround yourself with successful people, the kind of successful people who you believe in and, more importantly, who believe in you.

As you know, life does not allow you to pick your family, but it does allow you to pick your friends and work-related associates.

It is like in our garden at home. We select each flower for what it brings to the garden. Your mom and I choose the flowers, and thus we control the beauty of the garden everyone sees.

So if it is true that great minds do think alike, then choose to surround yourself with people whose minds can help you to become great, achieve great things, and to produce a beautiful result.

#212 ~ Accountability

Who are you accountable to for your own success? Is it your family, teammates, coworkers, your boss, or your friends?

The answer is yes, to all the above. Yet that list leaves out the single most important person to whom we all are directly accountable each day. Yes, you strive to impress the people around you. Yes, you desire their respect, approval, and admiration. You probably even believe, in most cases rightly so, that they all have your best interests at heart. Yet first, last, and always, you are, or at least you should be, accountable to yourself.

Maybe you would more clearly understand this fact if you thoughtfully answered the question, *Who else should care more about your success than you?*

Too often, we look the other way as we fail to give our best effort. Too often, we are dependent upon others to tell us what to do next. Too often, we fail to accept personal responsibility and accountability.

If you are to push through, you are the person you need to count on, even when your first inclination would let you settle for good enough.

You can only count on you, and in the end, if you have not met your goals, you have only let yourself down. How can you accept less than your best? How can you accept a result that is just good enough? Especially when you know that the person you are, should expect so much more.

#213 ~ Believe in Yourself

When you were a child, I would, oftentimes, ask you the question, "What are you?" The answer I had prompted you so often to repeat was, *The best!*

Maybe you never knew this, but your mom and I often fought over this parenting tactic. She felt that such pumping up would give you and your sister big heads. I have to admit now, that from time to time, I thought she might actually be right. As throughout the years, we often had to rein you both in so as not to let your egos overflow!

The point of the game was simple; I wanted to get you to believe in yourself. My thought here was that if you believed in yourself, you would be empowered to do anything you wanted. Looking back, I think it worked for both you and your sister.

This lesson learned as a child is a lesson that is not to be left behind in childhood. Today, as then, you are what you believe you are, and you are virtually powerless to achieve those things you believe not to be achievable. As a parent, by promoting and allowing you to believe in yourself, I gave you access to the most powerful force in humankind . . . *self-confidence!*

Successful people believe in themselves and their own limitless potential. This means that you need to wake up each day as you did when you were a child and know one thing . . . *You are the best!*

#214 ~ Patience Is a Virtue

When I was young and began to get antsy in anticipation of Santa Claus's arrival on Christmas morning, my mother would say, "All things in their time."

When I was impatiently awaiting the cookies to finish baking, my mother would tell me, "All things in their time."

Whenever I would start a sentence with the words *I wish*, my mother would remind me, "All things in their time."

It seemed like a *tough love* kind of lesson to a young boy. Yet the reality and the truth of her words are now clear to the much older me. In fact, I often laugh when I think what life would be like if the world was actually on my own personal schedule.

It is important to remember my mom's simple lesson when your plans do not bring about the desired result. Remember this lesson when your dreams remain unrealized no matter your efforts to reach them. Remember there is a certain satisfaction in knowing that, with your committed effort, all things are possible. That is, *all things in their time.*

#215 ~ Irrational Confidence

In order to find the success you seek, you must possess the strength of personality that shows itself as *irrational confidence*. That is, having within you, a level of personal confidence wholly different than the more common concept of self-confidence. The traditional thought of self-confidence is the kind of confidence that carries you forward always confident in what you know and fully confident in all the things that your own life's experiences have taught you.

On the other hand, irrational confidence is confidence in what is unknown. It is the fearless confidence that allows you to strike out in your own direction despite the fact that your final destination is completely unknown.

I define this irrational level of confidence as courage, the courage to step outside of your comfort zone. The possession of unwavering confidence in face of all that is unknown by definition has to be somewhat irrational.

You certainly must be able to muster the courage necessary in order to reach deep and take on all the challenges that each day presents. You need to be able to go forward with a confidence and self-trust. It is through that powerful combination that you will find within yourself the ability to make your effort a success.

#216 ~ Cheat the Inevitable

The inevitable does not have to be inevitable . . . That is why they play the game.

When faced with supposedly insurmountable odds against your being successful, look to be the *giant slayer*. David stood his ground in the face of Goliath and found his victory against what you imagine would have been his inevitable defeat.

It is a good thing you do not live in biblical times because there is no such thing as monsters. Today you only need to face down life's giant challenges that stand in your path. Know this, when in the face of such challenges, you are a giant slayer.

You just need to remember the fact that when you are up against the giant, you should see no challenge as insurmountable and no outcome as inevitable. That is, unless you choose to turn back in fear. Otherwise, the possibility of your success is always within your reach.

#217 ~ Redefine Success

You redefine success when, driven by your own personal vision, you are able to change what success should look like. Thus, changing what other people believe it to be.

Every situation is the opportunity to take on the challenge presented and make it your own by redefining excellence. It is like the advice given over and over by the judges on *American Idol,* "Make the song your own." When you are successful in making a challenge your own, you will have redefined for all what it takes to be successful.

The athlete that was at one time the greatest of all time is always replaced by the next and newest greatest that ever was. A person of such abilities is the one who was able to accomplish those things previously thought not to be possible. They are the ones that had the courage to take on and to beat the record that the experts thought would never be broken.

Through your efforts, you can redefine how those around you define what it is to be successful. In your doing so, by definition, you will be considered a success.

#218 ~ The Journey

Persuasion is not a destination, but it is a journey. It is a journey where you work to take someone with you from point A to point B. You should see it not as something that you do to those around you, but as something you do with them and for them. In essence, that journey will be the road you travel together.

It is, as I stated, a journey. A journey where persuasion only occurs when you take the time and make the effort to take those you wish to persuade along with you every step of the way.

It comes down to your ability to put yourself in another person's shoes and to see their world though their eyes.

Persuasion should never be a process where one person, with heels dug in, is dragged kicking and screaming against their will to accept a certain point of view. There should be no kicking and screaming involved in the experience. If the point you are trying to make has real value to the person or persons you are trying to persuade, then it is your personal responsibility to make clear that value. Persuasion only happens when you work hard to help others to see how what you want will benefit them as well.

#219 ~ The Crying Game

Waaaaa! Waaaaa! If you let it, life can become nothing more than a crying game that is void of accountability and void of responsibility.

People sucked up into the crying game prefer to look at life as outside of their control. They expect, and when they do not get, they fall into the pattern of looking to place blame, crying as it were. They look for an opportunity to place blame for their circumstances. That is, place it anywhere else but where the blame belongs. You probably already know that the responsibility for a person's circumstance rests on their own shoulders. Just as that same responsibility for where you are today rests on your shoulders.

Successful people don't cry over spilled milk. They accept responsibility and then clean up the mess before pouring another glass. Success is often only found after facing down failure and stepping up to pour yourself another glass of milk.

Crying, no one wants to hear it. Each of us has our own challenges to face. Remember the words from Frankie Valli and the Four Seasons . . ."Big girls don't cry!"

#220 ~ Be the Constant

In love, work, and in friendship, the deal maker and the deal breaker is you. Everything else around you is the X-factor. In this case, you must learn to be the constant.

Nothing is foolproof; no road is without bumps and curves. Yet as a person, you have the ability to make up for the inconsistencies that surround your relationships with your own personal consistency.

Know your product. That is, know yourself and project confidence in who you are and what you can do to enhance any relationship in any situation.

I had said in one of the previous books that I thought that everything was selling. In the context of that thought, as it relates to achieving success, I was generally referring to the need for you to sell your ideas. That is, you must be prepared to sell others on all the things that you believe in.

This idea takes that previous thought one giant step further. What are you selling? The answer is now clear; you should always be selling others on the real you.

#221 ~ There's Always a Cost

Some people think they can save money by doing nothing. That is, not spending any money on anything. Other people think they can save money through buying a certain product or service that brings benefit to their lives, that is to say, by doing something.

The point of this contrast is to let you know there is *always* a cost. That is, there is always a cost for you to do something, and there is always a cost for you to do nothing. You cannot escape the inevitable cost of your decisions no matter which way you decide.

The trick to successful decision making in the area of business or personal finances is to determine which decision will end up costing you more. That is either what you may plan to do or what you may decide not to do. With this kind of information, you can then make a better decision of which is best for you in terms of your return on that investment.

Not all decisions in life are about dollars and cents, yet many of the most important ones are. That is why it is important to take the time carefully to weigh your options, and you will be able to take the answers to all your decisions to the bank.

#222 ~ Look on the Bright Side

For years, people have been encouraged to *think positively!*

The reality is that a positive attitude can have an amazingly positive effect on your journey to become successful. That is because people want to hang with people who are positive. As everyone knows that happy, positive attitudes are contagious.

You know, you can actually spot the positive people. They are the ones in the middle of the crowd. All those people around them are just eager to be near them. I am not saying that they are necessarily the life of the party, but they certainly do have a positive influence on all those around them, and that spirit is contagious.

By thinking positively, you foster a powerfully positive perception about who you are, as seen by those around you. In addition, by staying positive, you never put yourself in the position of limited potential through a consistent dialogue of negative speak.

Let's just keep it simple. It is as I always say, "A positive person *believes*, while a negative person *doubts!*" This means that you will need to look on the bright side in order to find your greatest chance for success.

#223 ~ It's All Up to You

I guess there just seems to be no limit to the advice I have to offer. It is as I said in the very first book; some of these ideas will hit you as if they are a ton of bricks, and others will leave you wondering what your dad could possibly be thinking.

Well, that is the point of this effort. It is to get you thinking. Not just to do as I say but to listen to what I believe to be true and then decide if those same things are true for you and the person you want to become.

Throughout your entire life, people will feel free to offer you their advice. In the end, it is up to you to make your own judgments and to make your own mistakes.

Just because I say it is so does not make it true. Just because others have offered their own take on what you should do or how you should do things, does not mean you should heed their advice.

Only you are fully invested into who it is you will finally become. Only you reap the reward or suffer the consequence of what you decide.

So listen first, but then decide for yourself!

#224 ~ The Finished Product

People may wonder who you really are. In fact, you may even wonder from time to time if you know who you really are. Yet however deep that question may seem, the answer is as simple as looking at the experiences of the life you have lived.

In today's world, life may often appear to be just a string of unrelated news-hour sound bites. Yet in reality, each of our life experiences connects to the one that preceded it and to the ones that follow. Life's interconnectedness helps us define for ourselves who we are. It is like how you build the foundation of a house. We only can achieve a solid result brick by brick, row by row.

It is by the act of binding the bricks together that the mason is able to build something lasting. Just like the skilled mason, you are the architect of your own life and must be able to see the finished home in the pile of unconnected bricks. Each day you build your life one story at a time. You should see each experience for the value it brings to the person it helps you become. You did not just one day wake up as the person you are. You were put together one brick, one board, and one shingle at a time exactly the same way as contractors built the house you live in.

Life is an ongoing process of connecting unrelated experiences, putting them together one at a time in order to create something more valuable than any of the individual pieces.

#225 ~ Most Important

Take a moment to decide on the ten things that are most important to you in your life. When you have finished your list, you have created your own personalized definition of what success would look like for you.

In each of these books, I have talked about ideas I wanted to share with you about how to be successful. Yet in all these words, I have yet to define successfully what success actually should look like.

In the end, I think the definition part is up to all of us as individuals. No one can or should try to define for you the very things that are most important to you. Only you can forge your own brass ring, and only you can grab the ring through the accomplishment of the goals you set for yourself.

Success will always be elusive, but it will be impossible to obtain if you fail to define what it should look like in the first place.

#226 ~ Never Walk Away

When you find yourself in a position of responsibility, you will achieve your greatest level of success through your ability to delegate to others the elements of execution required to fulfill that responsibility.

As I have said before, delegation of responsibility does not allow for abdication of those responsibilities. When you are responsible, you are responsible . . . first, last, always! You cannot delegate away responsibility for those things for which you are accountable.

Yes, delegation is a tool that allows people to multiply themselves in order to facilitate the achievement of the goal. However, in the end, the person held accountable for the successful completion of the task is the person who must take ultimate responsibility.

When you accept responsibility, you must delegate your way to success as you cannot do it all yourself. Nevertheless, you must not lose track of the fact that you can never walk away, as you are the one who is ultimately responsible.

#227 ~ Think Again

When you start to believe you know, you had better think again.

Things in life are not always as they first appear. The golfer who gets confused by the tricky putt proves this idea true. Based on experience, the golfer was certain that the putt would break three inches to the left. However, as soon as he strikes the ball, it quickly becomes clear that it is going to break in a slightly different way.

To protect against overconfidence, the professional golfer often looks to draw on the experience of his/her caddie.

In real life, we find ourselves alone with the sole responsibility to size up a decision, and we can only look to rely upon our own judgment. We do not have a caddie there to carry our clubs. Therefore, we should not take the putt without first taking a second look.

As I have written these *thoughts* within each of your books, I am consistently forcing myself to second-guess the advice I give. I always read and reread, write and rewrite. I often think that I have finally put an entry to bed only to see the obvious error the next time I go over the text.

Confidence is a powerful tool on your quest to be successful. However, knowing that life is a lot like a tricky putt can help you to keep your confident self a bit more humble.

#228 ~ No Means More Than No

In life, the word *no* has many meanings.

It can mean . . .
"No . . . I don't know you well enough!"
"No . . . Can't you see I'm busy?"
"No . . . I don't want to think about it now!"

The word *no* can mean all of the above. Though, the underlying message of the word may simply be that the person who places this formidable obstacle in your path only needs more information. They need more information in order to understand why they should consider helping you to move forward by saying yes.

You see, the word *no* is the easy decision for a person who does not really know why they should say yes.

Do not take no for an answer when all they are saying is, "Give me the information I need in order to tell you yes."

#229 ~ One and Done

Success is a mountain we must climb over and over and over. Maybe the fact that we are always striving is the great part. Success is not one of those *one and done* or *been there, done that* kind of experiences.

We strive, we struggle, we progress, and we succeed. The process is one we experience repeatedly. Of course, it does not always end with your success as the result of the effort. That is the challenge in front of us, in front of you each day.

It is as I have always said, "Every day is an adventure!" Today we start, tomorrow we start again, and the process continues to repeat itself.

I want you to savor and celebrate each success knowing that, in that singular moment, you have arrived at your goal. However, you must know this; tomorrow you will again need to get up out of your bed and start again, as I am certain that tomorrow you will still have places you want to go.

#230 ~ Jet Stream of Doubt

You have heard it said, "You are what you eat." I do not know if that makes me a doughnut or not, but what we take in mentally every day does have a powerful effect on who we become.

You are stupid, you are ugly, you are lazy, and you are not creative. The real lesson here is that you are influenced both by what other people say you are, while at the same time, you are more powerfully affected by what you tell yourself.

So if your diet of self-talk is self-defeating, then how will you gain the success your words effectively work to deny you? It is not easy, but you will need to find the internal strength to ignore the negativity that others shower on you. Even more important is the need for you to get out of the jet stream of doubt when the criticism comes from within. That is an incredibly more harmful form of critique, a form over which you actually have total control.

Success might just be the act of turning one's back on the concept of failure. Words have the power, but only you have the power over the words you say to yourself.

That means you should pick your words carefully, and you'll find that you actually will have a say in who it is you will ultimately become.

#231 ~ Flex Your Will

As I have often explained to you throughout the process or writing these books, "Ultimately, your success will be found at the intersection of your personal will and your individual talents."

Human history is filled with stories of individuals who failed to live up to their potential. In many cases, they simply lack the personal will necessary to focus their talent on a goal.

History is also full of people who, through their sheer will, seemingly make the impossible, possible. That is, possible both for themselves and for others.

We are each born with certain talents and aptitudes. Just because we have no control over how we are born does not mean we cannot develop those attributes that will allow us to jump higher, run faster, and hit the golf ball farther. Those achievements are a function of will. God may not have given you the physical attributes, but He gives you control over your will to succeed.

In these books, I have talked about success in many ways. However, it is often hard to get one's head around the concept of being successful, as success does not have a single definition that is right for all people.

Remember, when you flex your will, you make all things possible. Then you can see firsthand how your God-given talents will help you write your own definition of success.

#232 ~ Good Things Will Come

Patience . . . just my personally typing that word on this page is almost sacrilegious. No one, to my knowledge, has ever accused me of being patient. I am thinking that it might actually be against my religion to be patient. (Just kidding!)

Yet they say that patience is a virtue, so that means it must be a good thing to have or to be. Yes, even I know that sometimes we will need to wait for good things to come to us. Nevertheless, having patience does not mean abdicating our responsibility for making the good things in our life happen all on our own.

Being proactive is taking control of the things you can influence in order to make positive things happen in your life. Being patient should be limited to your personal acceptance of the things you cannot control.

So be patient—good things do come to those who wait. However, should you find that the call for patience is nothing more than an excuse for inaction, then push forward. Push past those who sit content, waiting for their wishes to come true, and go all out in order to make your own dreams a reality.

#233 ~ So You Think You Know

The first time I made a major mistake in business, it was because I didn't know—*my lack of knowledge.* I just did not know enough to have made the decision in the first place.

The second time I made the same mistake, it was because I thought I knew—*my lack of understanding.* I just did not fully understand what I thought it was I knew.

There is an old saying, "What you don't know won't hurt you." That could not be further from the truth. I believe and have tried to convince you that, a lack of knowledge is only equaled by a lack of understanding as two major causes for failure.

Yes, we are talking about success in this book. Nevertheless, you cannot discuss one without consideration of the other. It is not that your success is an all-or-nothing situation. It is not that you either win, or you lose. However, achievement without knowledge is not a likely outcome, certainly no more likely than finding success without clear understanding of the factors that influence your desired outcome.

This makes your responsibilities in the decision-making process clear. Seek knowledge first, but never accept knowledge as the end-all since knowledge has no value without its full and complete comprehension.

#234 ~ Find It

One of my boss's high school basketball teams found itself behind with time running out and called a time-out. In the huddle, the coach challenged his team, saying that if they wanted to win tonight they were going to have to *find it!*

The *it* he referred to was that something extra we all keep stored deep down inside ourselves. The it he spoke of is that little bit of extra strength, skill, commitment, personal will, determination, or focus we are able to call upon and bring to the cause. We draw upon that inner strength when we are under pressure to achieve victory.

Do you know where you keep your it?

Maybe you summon your little something extra with a signal like the one used to signal Batman in Gotham City. Maybe you just reach down and flip a magic switch to turn your it on. Maybe you are just one of those people who rise to the challenge instinctually on their own.

No matter how you summon up that little bit extra, that sometimes we need in order to ensure victory, it is important that you get in touch with your own it factor.

Find it seems like good advice when faced with a daunting task. However, maybe the better advice is to *use it,* all the time. It is important to use all the tools within your ability to gain the victories you seek each and every day. Whatever you do, do not let yourself get into a situation in which you find that your time for victory is running out.

#235 ~ For Good or for Bad

The person you are is a composite picture of all you have experienced throughout your life. As individuals, we tend to judge those experiences, grading them on a simple scale from either good to bad.

Yet it is important to realize, as you look back at those experiences with an eye always toward tomorrow, that you know that you are who you are because of those experiences. You are not simply a product of the good times, but equally, you must realize that you are also a product of those not-so-happy times.

Remember this, if you like who you are when you look in the mirror, then you have those many tough times along with the good ones to thank for it.

Now what I hope this revelation does is to help you put into perspective all the challenges you will face going forward. You see, if you were not crushed by your past failures and unplanned detours, you will not likely be crushed by the challenges you will most certainly face in the future.

If the good person that you are has come, in part, from bad things you have experienced, then you must never forget that nothing, after all, can really be that bad!

#236 ~ The Game Isn't Over

"Strike one!" calls the umpire.

"Hey batter, batter . . ." The chatter from the field adds to the tension in the stadium.

A swing. "Strike two!" calls the umpire.

The crowd roars in anticipation of either the impending hit or the umpire calling the third strike.

Here is the pitch . . . a swing . . ."Strike three!" is the call. *You're out!* signals the umpire as the crowd goes wild.

This is a familiar scenario for any baseball player or fan.

Okay, so he struck out. That does not mean that the game is over or that he is out of the game. His team will get another chance to bat again next inning, and once they have batted around the order, he will get another shot too.

Life is a lot like baseball because in both instances, striking out is clearly not the end of the game. In baseball, a three-hundred hitter will probably be considered hugely successful and be paid a whole lot of money for his talents.

When you get up to the plate, do not be afraid to swing the bat and risk striking out, as you will not hit a home run with the bat resting on your shoulder.

#237 ~ You Can Run

I do not know where or when I first heard the idea, "You can run but you can't hide." However, to me, that is clearly an excellent articulation of many people's emotional response to personal failure. When many people fail, as we all inevitably will do from time to time, they just want to hide from that result.

Troubles will not and do not disappear just by turning your back on them; they will always follow you. Only by standing up and accepting this failure as your temporary result are you able to set aside a setback in order to get yourself back on track.

You will never have the opportunity to see the light at the end of the tunnel if you allow your fear to prevent you from going forward into the dark in the first place.

The light is there, even when it seems the darkest. You just have to trust me on this one!

#238 ~ You Decide

Who defines your efforts as a success? Oftentimes, those with whom you surround yourself out of their kindness and appreciation congratulate you. They will personally make an effort to comment positively on your achievement, your victory, your effort, or your skills.

Always be gracious in accepting their good wishes. Yet, I warn you not to be lulled to sleep by allowing others to define the parameters of your success for you.

Yes, you can and should appreciate their good wishes, but you are the one who sets your own bar. You evaluate, you are the judge, and only you decide if you have exceeded or even met your own expectations.

When you do measure up to the standard you have set, and you will, do not forget to be equally gracious with yourself. Take a moment to recognize your own accomplishments. You owe it to yourself to take a moment to celebrate each time you succeed!

#239 ~ There Are Signs

Navigational beacons mark the route of safe passage along the waterways. In life, our way is less clearly marked.

However, if you keep a watchful eye, you will see that there are signs to guide you through life as well. These are signs that will help you make the right choices to choose the right path. Like the highways we travel by car, life's highway is also marked by signage that is there to help guide our actions. Pay attention to the signs along the roads you travel, as you will certainly pay the penalty for not taking notice of the signs and following their advised course.

Try telling the police officer that you missed the change in the speed limit from forty miles per hour to twenty-five miles per hour. Try telling the officer that you did not see the stop sign at the intersection. When you miss a sign along life's highway, you will find your excuses ring just as empty.

That is why it is so important that you keep your eyes open and watch for the navigational beacons life has placed along your route. That way, you will never need to make excuses, as you will likely never run aground.

#240 ~ The Pilot Light Always Burns

On Grandma's old gas stove, if you got down close to examine the stove's burners, you could see that, tucked in the back underneath the stove top itself, the pilot light was burning.

The pilot light on that stove was kind of like the passion for living that burns inside you. That passion does not have to be an all-consuming flame. It does not always have to show up as an emotion you wear upon your outstretched sleeve. Yet like the pilot light, your passion is always there at the ready to fire up the inner drive to be successful, and that is what helps to make you who you are.

Turn on the burner of the stove, and the flame jumps to life, ignited by the little pilot light hidden away in the back. In your day-to-day living, when your ever-burning passion to achieve your goals ignites, its glow clearly is seen by all who know you.

What then is it that fuels your personal passion? I think you will find that it is when in life, you get to do what you love . . . every day.

It is that passion for having the opportunity to do what you love to do that fuels that ever-burning desire to succeed. It is that kind of passion that burns in your belly, as your desire to succeed is seen by others as the fire in your eyes.

It is that kind of passion that you can depend on to be your own personal pilot light.

#241 ~ The Art of Learning

An old axiom states that we are born with two ears and one mouth, and that means we should listen twice as much as we talk. This is especially true if we actually hope to learn something from the people around us.

Each day when we venture out into the world, we should look for the opportunity to learn something new. With that in mind, there is one thing I can promise you. That is, you will have no chance of learning anything when you are the one always doing the talking.

Listening is about more than just being quiet and waiting politely for your turn to talk. Listening is purpose driven. Listening is how you gain perspective, enhance your understanding, contemplate a point of view, or develop empathy for others.

Listening is not happening if you are always the one who is talking. Listening is not happening when your mouth is a missile waiting to launch. Listening is not happening when you are not even interested in what the other person has to say.

Suffice it to say, if you want to be successful, shut up and listen for once. You might just learn something!

#242 ~ Magic Words

As a child, I personally know that your parents worked hard to teach you the powerful magic words of *please* and *thank you*.

I would like to suggest to you that a person could not truly succeed in life without the knowledge of and commitment to use the single most powerful magic words in the sphere of intrapersonal relations. Those powerful magic words are the use of an individual's name.

I ask you, how good do you feel when someone you met just once or twice calls you by your name the next time you see each other?

If you want people to help you get what you want, then commit to give them what they want, the personal respect of remembering to call them by their name.

"Excuse me, sir. Do we know each other?"

#243 ~ Who You Know

It's not what you know, it's who you know. This socially accepted truism speaks to the power of a person's sphere of influence. Who is it that you know? Who is it that knows you?

In reality, you are like the hub of the wheel, which is referred to by many as your social circle. Within that circle, sociological researchers say, your wheel has an incredible two hundred and fifty spokes. That is, people with whom you have some level of relationship. This means you personally know two hundred and fifty people with whom you have some level of personal influence.

The reach of your influence is exponential as each of the spokes in your wheel is a hub of their own personal wheel, thus providing you the opportunity to multiply the reach of your influence to two hundred and fifty, times two hundred and fifty, times two hundred and fifty.

Maybe instead of calling it the sphere of influence, we should refer to the concept of our interconnectedness as your personal *web of influence.* Your personal web grows each day as your relationships reach out, crisscrossing and reconnecting in so many different ways with people from so many varying backgrounds.

Now go out and spin your own personal web of influence as you work with and through others to create a level of success that could only be achieved through the *power of the many.*

#244 ~ Appreciate the Positive

When we achieve the success we desire, it is probably a pretty good bet that we probably didn't arrive at that destination on our own.

A simple thing, perhaps the simplest thing we can do for those who helped us to arrive is to show appreciation for their time, personal support, and financial resources. Take a minute to take note of all those around you on your journey and make a point to acknowledge their efforts and contributions to your success along the way.

Appreciation can be the paycheck that ensures those who have aided in your success today will be there for you when you need them tomorrow and the next day.

You will find that acknowledgment of an individual's contribution to your result is necessary in order to remain *king of the hill.*

#245 ~ Strong as Oak

I'm still sort of moved by your
"my word is stronger than oak" thing.

—Jerry Maguire

If you remember this line from *Jerry Maguire,* the 1996 hit film starring Tom Cruise, you know that his character Jerry Maguire nearly lost everything because, as a sports agent, he took the word of the father of a potential client in place of a written contract . . . *Oops!*

So how strong is your word? Is it as strong as oak, or more like balsam wood? My grandfather, my mom's dad, lived and died on the strength of his handshake. He judged everyone by how they valued their word and how they lived up to that word.

What does it mean to you when you make a promise and seal the deal with your handshake?

Jerry Maguire's lesson is one we all should heed, get it in writing no matter how sincere the words. Yes, that is cynical, but more sadly than that, it is probably reality.

However, from you, I expect more. No, from you, I know that you expect more. I am lucky enough to have seen firsthand that your word is important to you. I have witnessed that it means something when you shake hands. Know this, based on what I have seen, your great-grandfather would be proud to do business with you.

#246 ~ How to Decide

There are the decisions we should make, and then there are the decisions we end up having to make. Who will judge the ultimate right from wrong? Well, the answer to that is probably everyone will judge. We all have opinions, and most of us are not shy about taking the opportunity to share them.

You have to wonder, of those people who judge us, who has the right to make that judgment? If you are religious, you certainly have heard the saying, "What would Jesus do?" Not to go religious on you, but I am guessing that Jesus is judging, and that his judgment would probably be right.

My point here is not to arm-twist anyone into positioning Jesus as your moral compass; it is only to strongly suggest that we all need some sort of a moral compass to guide us each day.

If everyone around us is sitting in judgment, then to whom should you look to for guidance? I suggest that, at the very least, you should always be your own judge.

It is sort of what I call the *gut check* rule. Ask yourself the question, *What would I do if my sole goal was, in the end, to be proud of my decision?* It is not that you do not want to win or to be seen as a winner. However, the answer to that question is more likely to be clarified by how you answer this question, *What price am I willing to pay in order to win?*

That, my dear, is a true gut check!

#247 - Glory or Goat

As a kid, you probably played the game Hot Potato. In that game, you passed an object around the circle. When the buzzer went off, you tried to avoid being the one left holding the *hot potato.*

It is kind of the opposite in the game of life. In life, someone has to step up if your team is to win. Someone has to be willing to grab the hot potato and take the last shot to try to win the game.

Glory or goat is synonymous with win or lose. We have all seen classic sports highlights shown again and again. Many times, we have seen one of Michael Jordan's game-winning shots played repeatedly on sports television. Each time you see his success, it builds on his legend. Much less documented, however, are the shots he took to win the game that bounced off the rim.

When the game is on the line, the great ones want to have control of their own and their team's destiny. When the game is on the line for you, you cannot perceive the responsibility for victory as a hot potato. To be a winner, it needs to be more like the kids' game of Musical Chairs where the objective is to be sitting in the last chair when the music stops.

Who is it that you can possibly trust to follow through, to do the job, to make it happen more than yourself? It is a measure of your confidence and your personal success to date if your answer to that question is *no one.*

#248 ~ It's Never Equal

Friendship is not likely to be the by-product of a carefully maintained accounting ledger. *One for me and one for you* may have been the best way for a couple of kids to split a bag of jellybeans. As their process of splitting required that the bags just had to be *equal*. The one for you, and one for me method of dividing the jellybeans was a great way to make sure it was *exact*.

Relationships based on scorecards that claim their ability to measure caring, friendship, and love are literally contradictions to the words. Love is a verb—it is something we do—it is not a place or a number. You cannot say you are in love in the same way you can say that you are in a puddle.

You can love, and you can care when you have freed yourself from the burden of the scorecard. The joy is in the giving, not in the process of tallying the score.

#249 ~ The Tiger Within

"Rising up, back on the street." Those words are from a hit song by the group Survivor, from the movie *Rocky III*. It continued, "Went the distance, now I'm back on my feet. Just a man and his will to survive."

Do you have what the song calls the *eye of the tiger?* Is your focus clear and your goal singular? Do you have the fight in you to get back up off the canvas when life knocks you down?

For decades since the movie came out, the words from that song have been burned in my psyche. The story in the movie is a simple one. It is about a young fighter who fought his way to the top only to lose focus and later fall from fame. That is until he found within himself the eye of the tiger, which enabled him to reach down inside himself and claw his way back to the top.

The moral of the story tells us that we each have a champion that lives inside of us. We just have to find our inner Rocky. Rocky rediscovered his heart, and that renewed passion carried him back to the top. With the searing focus of a hungry tiger, he did not let anything stand in the way of his efforts to reclaim his title as *champion*.

You need to find your passion, your eye of the tiger, and then get out of your own way as that passion for living will take you anywhere you want to go.

#250 ~ Have Faith

If you believe it—if you hold close philosophies of life which you promote—then you have to be willing to back them up with your actions . . . 100 percent.

I guess it is the *put your money where your mouth is* philosophy. You cannot be the successful person you want to be if you live a *do as I say and not as I do* lifestyle.

Where does respect come from? I would like to suggest it comes from having others see you as a person who actually does what they say they will do. You should lead by example, and then you will be able to live your life comfortably in the shadow of your own words.

To say that you believe something, then not to follow through on your own advice seems more than a bit hypocritical. How can you believe your suggestions will actually help others to succeed if you have so little faith in your own words that you consistently fail to heed your own advice?

Back up your words with actions and live what you believe, and you will find the success you seek. Show no doubt in the power of your words. Then through the confident execution of your actions, your words will take you further than you ever dreamed possible.

#251 - Excellence Is Your Work

Become known for what you know. When you seek excellence in your work, relationships, and everyday life, excellence becomes a habit. This is how you start the process in order to have others know you for what you know.

With excellence as a habit, that excellence begins to define you. It defines you not just by your own commitment to achieve excellence as it relates to all the big things. Moreso, you achieve the big things through your realization that excellence grows from how it is we do all the little things as well.

Understand that excellence is not just about good-better-best. When you have made excellence a habit, it helps you to focus all your skills and abilities in all your efforts to succeed.

Just wanting others to see you as excellent is not enough to begin to make it happen. The first step is to sit down and describe for your own self what excellence looks like. Be careful not to describe what perfection looks like, as pursuit of perfection can set you up for certain failure. Usually, the concept of perfection represents an unattainable standard for every one of us.

Start by drawing yourself a picture today and know that your pursuit of excellence does not stop with that one picture. As time goes by, it will always be necessary to redefine your standards, sharpen your pencil, and redraw your picture of what excellence looks like in your ever-changing world.

#252 ~ Winning Isn't Everything

I think it is fundamentally true that, if you do not take yourself seriously, no one else will. On the surface, I fully accept that premise. However, not without adding these two cents, "Just don't take yourself too seriously!"

If you are a heart surgeon, your failure is a life-or-death issue. If you are a lawyer trying a capital case, your failure could be a life-or-death issue for your client. It is hard to imagine that someone could take those responsibilities too seriously.

For the rest of us normal folks, failure is an option. That is because we get to pick ourselves back up and try again tomorrow. I am not saying put in no effort. I am not saying do less than your best. I am not saying to pack it in when the going gets tough.

What I am saying is that win, lose, or draw, life goes on! I am saying confidently that for most of us, we will live through our failures to fight another day. With all due respect to the great Coach Vince Lombardi's immortal words, "Winning isn't everything, it's the only thing," I think this takes it all a bit too seriously. As far as I know, the Green Bay Packers always have another game to play next week.

So don't beat yourself up, don't put yourself down, and do not take yourself too seriously. If you win, enjoy the victory. If you lose, prepare yourself for victory and a better tomorrow.

For tomorrow, you get a completely new set of downs, and the game begins anew. Tomorrow, it is first and ten, and you have the ball!

#253 ~ Success Can Be Fleeting

I know this concept will sound foreign to you sun worshippers, but there are those of us who when at the beach seek the shade under the nearest *palapa*. (That's Mexican for umbrella.)

That is my goal whenever we plan a trip to the beach. With that in mind, I pick my spot under the umbrella's shadow, position my chair, get out my reading glasses, and grab a good book. I then settle in . . . mission accomplished. That is, until the sun repositions itself, and the shade of the *palapa* shifts just enough to leave me no longer in the comfort of the shade I prefer.

That is how success is. It is like the bubble in the level, where just the tiniest shift of circumstances takes the bubble off center requiring us to make adjustments in order to get the level back to square.

I know you have heard the saying that *success is fleeting*. It is just like the shade covering my chair under the *palapa*. To maintain your success, you have to be ready, you have to be prepared to adjust your strategy. Just as I am always ready to move my chair in order to stay in the shade.

Sure, it is an ongoing battle to stay comfortable in the shade. Just as maintaining one's level of personal success is also an ongoing struggle. I can assure you of one thing. In the end, both of them are so worth it!

"Señor, *por favor*, can I get another margarita here?"

#254 ~ Tend Your Garden

To be successful in life, you must be successful in the cultivation of relationships. I love the use of the word *cultivate* in terms of how we create successful, mutually fulfilling relationships. Let me explain why.

Within our garden at home, we struggle to find the right plant for a specific location. Not all flowers thrive in a specific kind of light, not all plants can grow in certain types of soils, nor can all plants tolerate the same amount of water.

Just as we cultivate the flowers in the garden, we must cultivate the relationships in our lives. Each person is like the flower in that each needs to be tended in differing ways if the relationship is to bloom.

The first step in this process is to be aware and sensitive to the needs of the people around us. When you give a plant the right light, water, and fertilizer, you can help any plant to grow. The same is true for your relationships. Give a person enough time, space, love, empathy, compassion, support, and understanding, and your relationship with that person will grow.

Make note: It is all about giving first.

First, I water the garden, pull the weeds, put down the fertilizer, and lay in the mulch . . . Only then do I expect the flowers to bloom.

#255 ~ The Hurrier I Go

When I was ten years old, I started working in our family clothing business. One of the many lessons I learned from those years was from our store tailor. Her name was Claire, and she was a hard worker as were many of the tailors I had the pleasure to work with over the years. Claire was unbelievably calm, at least most of the time, in dealing with the pressure of her deadlines. Even way back then, everyone wanted it and needed it now or, should I say, yesterday.

Claire had this plaque, which she hung on the wall above her sewing machine. It said, "The hurrier I go, the behinder I get!" As a little kid, the word *behinder* always made me laugh, and I must admit as I write it now it again makes me smile. I digress.

The point of telling you this story is to warn you that the words on that plaque were true. Those words are just another way of saying that *haste makes waste*. It is just another way to tell the story of the tortoise and the hare. Proving once and for all that slow and steady does win the race. That does not mean being slow for slow's sake. It is more about the need for your efforts to be focused and deliberate.

Beware of the tendency to be sucked up into the rush of activity as deadlines approach only to then need to take those dreaded two steps back, due to the unforced errors you made under all the pressure.

So if you are going to do it, take the time to do it right the first time!

#256 ~ Extra Padding Please

When you were first learning to walk, for every step forward, there was a corresponding . . . *kerrrplunk!* Down you would go. Yet in the end, you learned to walk.

When you were learning to downhill ski, it seemed we spent more time helping you up than skiing down the hill. Nevertheless, you learned to ski.

Do you remember little Greg Horant? When you kids were little and learning to ice-skate, he fell down so much that I nicknamed him *Crash.*

What I am saying is that if you are not falling, you are not learning. When you live life within your limits, when you fail to test your talents by taking them to the edge, you are likely never to fall. As I've seen so many times, learning is to be found in the experience of falling.

The greatest accomplishment for you would be one day to earn for yourself the nickname . . . Crash. Because it was not in the falling that little Gregger earned his nickname. For me it was in his eagerness to always get back up and try again.

#257 ~ One Bad Apple

Beware of the power of the bad apple. The saying goes, "One bad apple can spoil the whole bunch." The power of the bad apple says that the one has the power to destroy the many. One rude person, one unreasonable customer, or one unruly child can all change your perception of your day. That is, if you let them.

Just as one apple negatively affects the others, you only need to remove it from the basket to take away its power to influence the group. Even though we cannot pluck the *negative-nellies* from our life and the world around us, we can minimize their power over us by putting them and their stupidity into perspective.

By keeping that one bad experience in perspective within the course of our day, we do not let it cloud over all that was positive during the rest of our day.

As radio legend, Paul Harvey, says, "And now you know . . . the *rest* of the story." He was always able to change how we thought and how we saw things simply by providing us with additional information, allowing us a view of events from a different perspective, allowing us to form a different conclusion.

Do not allow your daily story to be written from a single perspective. To do so could take away your story's happy ending.

#258 ~ It Happens

If the inevitable is inevitable, how is it that we are so often surprised when the inevitable actually happens?

There are those among us who boast about their eternally optimistic view of life. They like to call themselves the *glass is half-full* crowd. I might suggest politely they be called the *head in the sand* society.

The bumper sticker says it all, "Shit happens." So why would that surprise anyone?

Why do we cry over spilled milk when spilling the milk is a likely and possible result of having poured it in the first place? Some things are just inevitable. Here is a short list of other of life's inevitabilities: A teenage driver will crash the family car. Investments will lose money over specific periods. Spaghetti sauce will splatter on a white shirt. You will miss an appointment due to traffic conditions.

I am a realist; your mom says pessimist. Knowing and admitting that bad things happen to good people is not being pessimistic. I think it is just my own pragmatic view of world events. It then is just a matter of keeping these events in perspective.

Of course, I hope for the best. I too enjoy looking on the bright side. It is just that I hedge my bets on the possibility, no, should I say, the probability that bad stuff can happen. This way I will always be ready!

#259 ~ Silence Is Less than Golden

Say nothing, and I can assure you that you will most certainly fail to inspire those around you by your silence. Words are the language for your ideas. When you fail to share what you think, your ideas can provide others no hope, motivation, or direction. An idea not shared is of no benefit to anyone.

When you feel that it is fear that keeps you from unleashing the power of your ideas, push back against the fear. Know that even though others may disagree with your ideas, their correction, criticism, and critique can never hurt you, those things only represent their opinion.

Do not use this fear as justification for your silence as differing ideas and opinions will never hurt you. Know that often it is the individual who is without ideas of his/her own that finds their only option is to build themselves up by criticizing the ideas of others. (Think politicians.)

I urge you to share your ideas knowing for certain that those are the ideas, that in time, will surely help you achieve the success you deserve.

#260 ~ Clear Your Calendar

Give yourself the space you need in order to be *great*. To do that, clear your calendar for an hour a day or even a day a week. When you take the time to clear your mind, you will be surprised at how creative you become. Clear your calendar to give yourself time to go for a run, ride a bike, or lay in a hammock in order to watch the clouds go by. Within this gift of a mental time-out is your opportunity to think clearly.

Most, if not all, of what was written here for you was not written by me on a time schedule or done as a task. I did not sit down saying to myself, *be creative, be insightful, be inspiring*. No, almost all of these thoughts came to me when I was not so much thinking about anything. (Which your mom says happens with me a lot.)

Now given the sheer number of entries in these books, one would assume that I have a lot of free time. That is not true. These ideas came to me prior to falling asleep or just after awakening in the morning. These thoughts came to me while I was working in the garden, exercising, or while on the phone waiting on hold for a customer.

My point is that your imagination is not a trick pony ready to perform on command. This means that when you have a challenge that seems to have no easy answer, I give you permission to get up and run away from it all. I promise the solution will surely catch up with you sooner than later.

#261 ~ Stay in School

I think that fish swim in schools because they are smart enough to know that if they stay close, they can learn a lot from those around them.

Are you smart enough to learn many of life's lessons from the good people around you? The fact is you do not have to experience everything firsthand in order to say that you have learned from experience. You do not have to hit your head on the same wall as I did in order to see that the bump on my head signals to all that the wall is hard. The lessons—learned by those with whom you surround yourself—can be every bit as valuable as the lessons you have learned by your own efforts and mistakes.

Be smart enough to know that if someone tells you do not touch the stove, it is probably hot. You do not have to learn that lesson for yourself.

Yet not all that we are told can, or should, be taken at face value. The best advice is swim with fish who you admire, look up to, trust, and respect. Based on the reliability of their advice, you can confidently say that you have learned from *their* lesson.

#262 ~ Imaginary Money

You can spend it, but you cannot touch it. You can spend it, but you cannot put it in your wallet. You can spend it, but you cannot deposit it in the bank.

If-come is income you have yet to earn, and it only becomes real income if certain things happen. If-come is not real, at least not yet, and maybe never will be. Nevertheless, the trouble caused by the uncertainty of your spending money you only hope you will one day have . . . is *real!*

Despite the dangers, many people bet on the future and the income they hope to generate. Planning life around money you have yet to make is like playing house with imaginary friends. You would think that we all feel foolish if others caught us playing house with imaginary people. Despite that, we still go forward and spend the money we don't yet have.

Resist the urge to make commitments based on what may never be. Live life based on the reality of what is real, and that is your income.

You should know that the money you hope for might never come. Yet the commitments we make in spending it are real, and they can come back to haunt us. I think we all understand the concept of *easy come, easy go* when it comes to money. The problem is that for most of us, money does not come easily. We must work for it, and most people work hard.

Just remember that your if-come is easy go, easily gone. That is probably because when money is not real, and when you have not yet worked for it, you will find that it is easy to spend all your pretend money.

#263 ~ It's What You Give

Some define success by what they get from life. In other words, the things we all collect along the way define it. Yet our satisfaction with life is measured more often by what it is that we give back.

When we believe in the Lord's *Golden Rule* of do unto others from Matthew 7:12, one cannot help but understand the importance of how it is we chose to help others in this life.

I have long believed in the idea that "you can *take* satisfaction in the glow of your achievements, but you are *given* satisfaction when you give of yourself to others."

We should base the true measure of a person or of their personal success upon what it is they do for others. You do not have to be rich to give. You just must have been born with a heart of gold.

That means that it is not about how you are paid, but it is all about how you pay back that defines your success.

Remember, every day of your life is a gift—find a way to repay the generosity!

#264 ~ Be Careful

I have said it over and over, mostly in a joking tone, "Be careful what you wish for, you might just get it." This implies that what you are wishing for might just not be everything you were hoping for.

Just as every coin has two sides, so does every outcome. Your dream of one day having your boss's job may leave you without the free time you treasure. While at the same time, you may have your wish granted for more time off through fewer responsibilities and end up with a decreased feeling of personal accomplishment in your job.

There you are, *damned if you do and damned if you don't*.

Let us go back to where we started, *be careful!* What more could I possibly say on this topic? I have been telling you this for your entire life. Unfortunately, I know that like most kids, you often ignore your father's advice. I must admit that I never followed many of my own father's similar warnings. I guess at that time, I just didn't think he was all that smart. You will find it amazing as to how smart your parents become as you get older.

Yet my thought here is a different kind of warning. Maybe I could more positively make my point by telling you to be careful to know and understand what you are wishing for and why you're wishing for it. If you make this effort and then you end up getting it, you might just be happy.

#265 ~ Affecting Change

As you get older, you realize that there are many things in life that will not go your way. Additionally, you will find that a huge number of requirements and rules just do not seem fair.

I suggest you make a list of all these things. I do not need a prioritized list but just a list of the stuff you feel is not right. Make it ten to twelve things long. Go ahead and do it now, or you probably never will. I will wait.

Now read your list and ask yourself which of these things you can actually change. When, in this process, you come across something that you cannot effectively change, cross it off your list. Use a heavy black marker so you cannot read it or think about it again. Those things you have crossed out are the things that do not really matter. They do not matter because you cannot change them anyway. Now title your new, shorter list, *The Things I Can Change*.

What is left on your list? It's the stuff you should be worried about; this is the stuff where your efforts at change will give you a chance to make a difference.

The rest of that stuff is just crap you cannot change, no matter what you do. So why waste your time in what is certainly a fruitless effort? You should realize that complaining and affecting change both require your time and energy. However, only one of them improves your life or the lives of those around you. The other does not.

So what are you waiting for? Quit complaining about that which you cannot change and start changing the things you can.

#266 ~ Do As I Say

I should have thought about titling the combination of all these books, *A Hypocrite's Guide to Success: Do as I Say, Not as I Do.*

I read a story from the book *Go-Givers Sell More* by Bob Burg and John David Mann. The story tells of an encounter between a mother and her son with Indian leader Mahatma Gandhi. The mother had come to Gandhi to ask him to tell her child not to eat sugar. Oddly, Gandhi instructed her to go back home and return in thirty days. Upon her return, Gandhi did as the mother had asked and told the child not to eat sugar. When asked by the mother why she had needed to travel home and then return after thirty days, Gandhi's reply was, "I first needed to stop eating sugar."

As your dad, I am taking the parental way out and asking you to consider doing as I say and not so much as you have seen me do.

There are great coaches in sports who, at one time, were great players like Mike Ditka in football. Then there are great players like Larry Bird in basketball, who never made great coaches. Yet the proof in the power of *do as I say* is based on the respect earned by the legendary coaches who never played their game at its highest levels, coaches like Red Auerbach who led the Boston Celtics basketball dynasty. For Coach Auerbach, his do as I say knowledge made his players into champions.

So trust me on some of this, and for just this once, do as I say.

#267 ~ Look Out for the Wolf

Imagine how it would be if a home could be built by constructing the roof first? If this were possible, upon what would your roof rest?

What would happen if you decided that you wanted to build the walls of your house first? Upon what would those walls stand?

It is clear to me that you build a strong house from the foundation up. Like a house, you too should build your success in life from the ground up. Lay the foundation for your success first by doing your homework, paying your dues, and taking advantage of all the opportunities made available for you to learn.

Realize that it is only a strong foundation, which you built yourself over time, that will have the strength to sustain you when the big bad wolf starts huffing and puffing and tries to blow your house down.

#268 ~ Listen to the Answers

Having the opportunity to have your performance judged without prejudice is important. Having the ability to accept the criticism that goes with that process is critical to your long-term success.

It is important that you be able to recognize the difference between those who offer you *constructive criticism* versus what could be termed *destructive criticism*. To survive the process, you must have broad shoulders, an open mind, and thick skin. This way, you can protect yourself from falling prey to the personal doubt that can result from such caustic levels of personal critic.

Sugarcoating of the truth by others as it relates to your strengths and weaknesses may make you feel better, but it will never help you be better.

It is like the Jack Nicholson line from the movie *A Few Good Men*, "You want answers . . . You can't handle the truth!"

If your goal is to improve, you must accept the answers to the questions you ask and then be able to handle the truth. Only by consistently seeking honest critique can you see clearly the road map to reaching your personal potential through the changes others say are needed.

#269 ~ You Are Who You Are

People are who they are and who they are seldom has anything to do with you. So why do we tend to take their unpredictable behavior so personally?

You did not cause those people to be short fused. You did not cause them to be sullen. You did not cause them to act out. So do not give them the ability to cause you to feel bad by internalizing those negative feelings triggered by their momentary mood swings.

You are no more responsible for people's changing personalities and resulting actions than you are for the minute-to-minute changes in the weather.

How, you may wonder, does this observation relate to achieving success? It is my guess that successful people have learned not to take other people's emotional responses personally. They have learned that the changing weather of human personality is unpredictable, and they do not accept responsibility and thusly do not end up feeling bad based on what they cannot control.

Learn to keep it all in perspective. Remember that an emotional response is all about the other person and that it is not about you. You just have to keep it all in perspective.

#270 ~ I'll Do It Later

Let me define procrastination as: *the developed and practiced ability to put off until tomorrow those things that are not as important to you as are the things you choose to do for yourself today.* (Great definition, isn't it? It kind of helps soothe my occasional guilt.)

When you accept yourself as a procrastinator, as defined above, it means you have empowered yourself. From today forward, you choose. From today forward, it is up to you to prioritize what comes first in your own life. As a procrastinator, you get to choose what you will invest your time in, both today and tomorrow.

In order to learn to accept the procrastinator label with a degree of pride, you need to accept that you cannot do it all. Nor, if you are honest, do you want to hold yourself responsible for doing it all. Nor will you allow anyone else to hold you responsible for doing it all against your will.

Yes, your job has things you must do in order to keep it, and your daily life has things that need your attention if you are to live it. After that, what is left for you? Where does the satisfaction of your own wants, needs, and desires come in? If you totally are invested into getting it all done, where will that leave you?

You will not find happiness in your opportunity to check another thing off your list. To feel truly successful, stop focusing on what others want and take a minute of time for what is important to you.

Just do not procrastinate when it comes to going after those things that make you happy!

#271 ~ Resetting the Bar

Perhaps you have yet to work for a demanding boss. Maybe you got through school without coming across a truly demanding teacher. However, I do know that you grew up with demanding parents, and I am fairly certain that it didn't kill you.

Demanding can be positive, or it can come across as negative if it is not motivated by the right reasons. For the purpose of this discussion, I will simply define a demanding person as one who raises the bar for you by expecting just a little bit more than you might naturally expect from yourself.

If you could run the mile in 4 minutes, then it would not be destructive for the coach to raise your bar to run the mile in 3:59. Now if that level were the height of the bar that someone set for me, well, that expectation would be crazy and destructive to my motivation to be a better runner.

Expecting your best and working with you to redefine what that means is by definition, demanding. However, that is only demanding in terms of a specific expectation's ability to help you to see that higher level of success as possible.

No one wants to feel trapped in an overly demanding environment, a destructively demanding environment. Therefore, when you are being pushed to be your best, resist human nature to push back and instead step up in order to push forward.

Besides, in the end, you should be the person who demands the most from yourself, and there is nothing wrong with that.

#272 ~ Don't Throw Stones

Let he who is without sin cast the first stone.

—John 8:7

We all are marked by our own imperfection, and the sooner you realize that, the happier those around you will be.

What do I mean by those around you?

We are all so fast to cast judgment on other people. We judge their intelligence, their attitude, and their actions. Yet those who live in glass houses should not throw stones. Judging, in and of itself, perhaps is not the bad part. Yet not trying to control your own natural human tendency to express those value judgments is the bad part.

The single question that comes to mind, as it belies the underlying issue here is, *Who are you to judge?* We have all behaved in ways that open ourselves to the judgment of others. Yet for most of us, though we can certainly give it out, we are sorely inadequate when it comes to our ability to take it.

"Judge not, that ye not be judged." These words from Matthew 7:1 are, to me, some of the most powerful and ignored in the Bible.

So let me say it, so you understand it. "If you don't have something nice to say, don't say anything at all."

#273 ~ Never Done

Many jobs are never finished, and even if you worked twice as fast or twice as many hours, you would actually never be finished.

So how do you know when to go home at night? How can you know when to stop for the day? Well, since you are like me in that our jobs do not have a daily finish line, I say go home when you are tired. Go home when your eyes glaze over and when your stomach starts to rumble. Because when the gas tank is empty, it is time to regroup for tomorrow.

Yes, there are jobs where the clock marks the day's starting and stopping point. In those jobs, people do what they can to accomplish all they can in the time allowed. Within those defined parameters, individuals will succeed, or they will fail.

Your mom and sister are both teachers, and the clock officially marks the end of their school day. Yet as you know, they have never let a time clock limit where they chose to set the bar for themselves.

Your own work time is limited, by the hours your customers choose to work. Yet the clock does not clearly define what is necessary in order for you to succeed. You need to know that excellence, for people who seek more for themselves, is not definable by the set hours on your watch.

So I say work until you are tired, rest, and then it will be time to work again.

#274 ~ Pay Attention

When you need help to succeed, ask for help. When you become lost, ask for directions. That is just as true when in a new town as if you are up against a new challenge for the first time.

What is important here is to remember that when you ask for help, consider the concept of actually listening carefully to the advice that is given. Now this is not to suggest that all the advice you will get when you ask will be good advice. It is not to say that you should accept that advice without close evaluation of the validity of the advice given.

For me, the biggest value of advice from others is that it comes to me from a perspective that is different from my own. Now I have filled this entire set of books with many pieces of advice. Some, but not all, of which is certainly powerful, relevant, and correct. The important thing to understand is that the value of my advice, like the advice solicited from others, is that it offers you a view of your situation from a different perspective. No matter what you achieve in life, your experience will often teach you differently than mine has taught me.

My advice, and you did not ask for it, is to remember that if you are going to ask, be smart enough to give their answers to your questions your full consideration.

#275 ~ You're Not Bored

There are many things your mom and I never let you do while growing up. Maybe one of the most important rules we set early on was, "Don't tell us you're bored."

"There's no one to play with, I'm bored!"

"School is too easy, I'm bored!"

"There's nothing good on tv, I'm bored!"

Being bored gives responsibility to someone other than yourself for making you who you are. We believed that success would come from one very important thing. That was from the realization that there was always something new to learn in any situation.

Because of that lesson, you now understand that it is your responsibility to find the joy in every moment. You understand that only boring people get bored. We never chose to let you consider any option other than the acceptance of your responsibility to take advantage of every opportunity as they presented themselves.

You now know that if you are waiting for someone else to entertain you, then you will not be bored, you will be boring.

#276 ~ You Can't Overthink It

I remember a time when I was too dumb not to succeed. I know that does not make much sense. The reality is, the more we know, the more we think we know. Of course, being so darn smart, we then are inclined to let that confidence get in the way of what is possible, all because we are certain that we now know better.

Certain traits and certain behaviors that have led you to your current level of success end up getting pushed aside by what you now think you know.

The mistake we often make is in our tendency to ignore the instinct-driven knowledge that has led to our current success. The act of overthinking your life has the potential to lead you away from those actions that helped you to produce your best results. There is a time within any new endeavor where you only can react. You don't yet know enough to get in your own way, so you react.

Just be careful to avoid the situation where the things that helped you to achieve your success worked so well, that in your real ignorance, you stopped doing them.

#277 ~ Anyone Can Think You're Right

No matter what you do or what it is you say, you cannot win them all. Accept it and get over it. A person could end up elected the president of the United States without gaining the support of the majority of voters, but when all is said and done, they are still the president.

When I moved to Eagle River, Wisconsin, to run one of our family businesses, my uncle warned me *not* to get involved. "It's a small community," he said. "For every person who thinks you are doing something right, there will be two of them who think you're doing something wrong."

Well, he was right, not with his advice about not getting involved. However, he certainly was right about his projection that two out of three people will be likely to disagree with your efforts to make any changes.

You will not win every argument, just as you cannot make everyone like you. That being said, you should not let that stop you from always trying to make a difference in the lives of those people around you.

#278 ~ Catch the Wave

The story of success is like the story of the waves in the ocean. The water comes in, and then the water goes out.

In my first job out of college, my new company was going to fire me after my first two weeks on the job. A fellow salesperson told me that he had overheard that conversation between my bosses, so I confronted them, asking what I was doing wrong. They told me, "You're not selling enough!" What a shock.

After my second month with the company, I was the region's salesperson of the month. In two short months, I had seen the waves come in and go out several times. Prior to my promotion as a manager of one of the company's stores, I was salesperson of the month in our region, five of the nine months I worked there and won four other selling awards during that time as well. I loved those waves!

In my second job, I was managing a men's clothing store. As Christmas approached, the owner asked if I would go to their highest grossing store to help boost sales. As it was an opportunity to earn some extra money over my management pay, I said sure. Then when the Christmas season ended, they asked me to take a lie detector test. You see, in that four-week Christmas period, I had sold twice as much in that period as anyone who had ever worked for the store. Of course, I passed the test, but the wave had come in, gone out, and rolled in again.

When I left our family business to go into managing radio stations, the owner fired me after five years. I guess I pushed my people too hard. Yet six years later, I ran into the owner of that station in a local parking lot just after she had sold her radio stations in order to retire. She called me over and said, "I just need to tell you something. I credit only two people in my life with my success in radio, and one of those is you." The waves go out, and the waves come in.

I later went to work as the general manager of another radio station in the same market. It was a great challenge as the station was brand-new, but it had been put together with glue and duct tape. Yet by the end of the fifth year, we were on track to generate more revenue than my old station was generating as the most profitable in the market. The wave had definitely come in, only to go out when the owner fired me. Again, I guess I was a bit too intense for everyone's taste. (There is probably some lesson there if I would only learn it.)

A year later, I decided to stop to see that radio station's owner at one of his stations in another town. You see, another wave had come in as I had just finished the first nine months with my new company and sold more in that time than anyone else in the company history had in their entire first year. I was definitely riding the wave. But then an even bigger wave hit when that owner admitted that since I left, my old station was down 25 percent. Big wave . . . big smile.

Success comes, and success slips away as the wave washes back into the sea. The moral of these stories is that success is like surfing. You ride the wave as far as it will take you and then you hop off the board to paddle back out and catch the next big wave. Surfers and successful people know there will always be another wave, and they are in position ready to catch it when it comes along.

#279 ~ What Is Important

We often find that we are impressed by our own exploits, by our efforts. We enjoy putting ourselves front and center and tend to see the world only as it applies to us.

Successful people have something so many others lack—that is their perspective. Sit back and examine one of your last conversations with a friend, coworker, or family member. Does it pass the *so what* test?

Everyone's favorite topic to talk about is himself or herself. Most everyone's least favorite activity is listening to someone else go on about themself. To avoid that trap and to help you develop a perspective about what is or is not important to others, try screening your conversations through the *who cares* filter.

Does anyone else care that much about what you are talking about? We already know you care and that is not to say family, friends, and coworkers are not happy to share in the joy of your personal success. However, at some point you need to realize that others may just not care all that much.

The sooner you realize that you are not necessarily at the center of the entire circle of life, you will then have developed the perspective of seeing things through the eyes of other people.

#280 ~ Out of the Pain Comes the Joy

On April 1, 2010, I called my mom to wish her a happy birthday. Of course, you know that day is not my mom's birthday. It is, however, mine. Since we were on vacation, and she could not call me to say happy birthday, I thought I would call her.

I think she appreciated the call. I told her I had called to thank her for all her sacrifice. I wanted to tell her how much I appreciated all that she had given me over the years.

To mark this last entry of your gift, I thought I would share her response. You know, to pass down the wisdom from generation to generation to you.

My mom told me, "There was no sacrifice. When they first hand you your baby, and they are perfect, all the pain goes away." She continued, "Sure, there were bumps along the road, but upon seeing that your child has successfully arrived, the memories of the bumps fade away, just like the pain of childbirth."

So there we have it, our long sought-after answer to the question of what is it that really defines success . . . *It is being loved!*

Up until this entry, I had written you 279 times about the concept of achieving success. All of them without yet being able to clearly define what success should be. I have very much implied the entire time that the definition of the word is up to you. In all this time, I had no idea that there was a possibility that a single definition might exist.

What more can be said about success than those five simple words from the legendary Beatles.

All you need is love!
—Lennon and McCartney

With love, you have everything you need to feel as though you have it all. Not money, not possessions, and not awards or recognition for your accomplishments can replace how the feeling of knowing that you are loved is able to help define you as a person.

Seek success in all its forms, but never lose sight of the fact that true success is nothing more than loving someone without reservation and being loved unconditionally for the person that you are.

When you were born, I remember telling your mom that I had realized something very important through the experience of the birth of your sister and you. I told her that now I know how much my parents love me. You kind of know as a kid; but until you feel for yourself the total, unconditional, instantaneous love for your own child, I don't know how a person can ever know how much love is humanly possible.

Let me tell you something now that I do not want you ever to forget. That is, *You most certainly are loved!* Knowing for certain, without doubt, means that you will never again need to ask yourself the question, *Am I successful?*

Out of pain of childbirth comes the joy of knowing you are forever loved . . . You are perfect . . . You are a success!

Epilogue

If you only read my dad's words once, there is no way they will have the same profound effect on your definition of success and your ability to achieve it as they have had on mine. Over the years, I have had many chances to read and reread all my father's books, "Success," "Next Level," "View from the Top," and "King of the Hill." In doing so, I experienced firsthand the underlying power of repetition in learning. Dad was right in his suggesting that my life's experience would reshape my perspective and, over time, allow me to find new meanings within his words.

If you only read these books once, you may not pick up on the powerful nature of his books' recurring themes: love, focus, hope, integrity, honesty, commitment, challenge, hard work, planning, positive thinking, judgment, perception, relationships, learning, achievement, challenge, give-and-take, empathy, communication, passion, unselfishness, risk, value vision, overcoming fear, winning, execution, goals, excellence, introspection, consistency, self-confidence, potential, adversity, courage, choices, respect, drive, motivation, sacrifice, creativity, struggle, opportunity, investment, responsibility, balance, aspirations, boundaries, attitude, self-determination, expectations, obstacles, persuasion, knowledge, conviction, ambition, ethics, independence, leadership, adaptability, persistence, loyalty, perspective, growth, preparation, interdependence, awareness, differentiation, empowerment, tenacity, and yes . . . even failure.

All these themes and the repetition with which they have been presented have allowed my dad to make clear to me the ideas that he hoped would chart my future. If I had only read his thoughts once, I would not have learned them, and they would not have changed me as they have.

Many times, you may have noticed that he again picked up one of his themes, though he had already touched on it several times before. If he thought the lesson important, he did not give up. Repeatedly, he would try to get his ideas across using different stories to make his point. All this planned repetition was to ensure that when I finished reading, I would have a clear understanding of his key underlying messages and beliefs. For example, we can all agree that the concept of commitment is important in achieving success. Just see if you can tell how important my dad thinks it is by counting how many times you find the word *commitment* within these four books.

As a teacher, my mom taught me that a key element in being a successful educator is your ability to take each opportunity given in order to emphasize your message. Many things must be repeated numerous times before they can be said to be learned. Within these pages, my dad focused on many themes and repeated their importance in order to help me learn that lesson and achieve the success he envisioned for me. It is as I said in a personal letter to my father (which you read at the beginning of this book), "What started out as your words of advice became my words to live by . . . They became part of who I am and how I endeavor to live my life."

Let me then close with a few words from my foreword to the book, "I know now more than ever that much of what he's written here has the power to change a life . . . That is because his words have changed mine."

Thank you for taking this journey with my dad and me!

—Kristine Pokrandt

Edwards Brothers, Inc.
Thorofare, NJ USA
November 7, 2011